STOP
STARVATION
MARKETING

23 Power Growth Moves
for Health Tech, IT,
Biotech Companies

STOP
STARVATION
MARKETING

CHRISTINE SLOCUMB

INDIE BOOKS
INTERNATIONAL

CONTENTS

FOREWORD

STOP STARVATION MARKETING

As a healthcare IT journalist and founder of the Swaay Health (formerly HITMC) marketing community, I get to see the good, the bad, and the ugly when it comes to the world of healthcare marketing.

When I look at some of the campaigns, PR outreach, websites, and other marketing efforts from companies in the space, it is no wonder why they are not finding success. This is a travesty since many of these companies have great solutions that could improve the lives of patients and clinicians. However, their marketing falls so short that they never find commercial success.

Improving marketing is about improving communications and understanding the customer's needs. This pragmatic book is filled with solid tactics, practical tips, and real-world case studies to help companies share their message through best-in-class marketing.

If you are a company leader in the health technology, IT, and biotech space, you need to influence many audiences: clinicians, patients, caregivers, health system leadership, and end users.

There are no impulse buys by an individual in healthcare. If you do not influence all these stakeholders, any one of them could ruin your sales efforts. Effective marketing is the only way to influence the committee of buyers in healthcare at scale.

For anyone aspiring to improve your marketing frontiers, you will find something of interest in these pages. The power moves detailed in this inspiring and advice-filled book can help transform your marketing.

Sadly, many companies with great technology are starving their marketing and communications efforts. In healthcare, the real losers are the patients who may never obtain the technologies that could help them. Healthcare needs you to be successful in your healthcare marketing efforts.

The author, Christine Slocumb, suggests this is a fixable problem since she has seen the solution firsthand. This is the first book I have seen that truly explains how marketing works for health tech businesses and how the lessons can be applied to your company.

Plus, Christine understands the value of power moves. I first met Christine when she did the power move of submitting a speaking session for my healthcare marketing conference to the non-existent call for speakers. This kind of bold but thoughtful thinking is what is illustrated throughout the book.

Thanks, Christine, for providing a structured framework for companies that are struggling in their marketing efforts and for sharing your insights on the importance of properly feeding marketing campaigns. Many important products and services fail to reach their full potential because the leaders underfed the efforts to get the word out. This is a masterful job of distilling three decades of wisdom into a highly readable book.

As a fellow journalist and short story writer Damon Runyon quipped, "The race is not always to the swift nor the battle to the strong, but that's the way to bet." In Christine's words, "Betting only on the best tech leads to a trainwreck." Don't overestimate the value of your technology and underestimate the importance of marketing and communications.

John Lynn

Founder, Healthcare Scene, which includes the Healthcare IT Today and Swaay Health Communities

PREFACE

Back in 1898, an advertising executive named Elias St. Elmo Lewis cooked up the first sales funnel graphic and called it "The Purchase Funnel".[1] And now, your sales and marketing teams are still clinging to it like it's the only life-boat on the Titanic. They probably even use it to impress the board saying: "Look, we have a colorful funnel graphic with numbers on it, we're so amazing!"

THE PURCHASE FUNNEL CIRCA 1898

Awareness — MARKET POTENTIAL

Interest — SUSPECTS

Desire — PROSPECTS

Action — CUSTOMERS

Your customer journey isn't a linear funnel; it's more like a wild roller-coaster ride full of twists and turns. Business-to-business (B2B) buyers are like detectives, consuming more evidence than Sherlock Holmes before making a decision.

In fact, they consume an average of thirteen content pieces before making a purchase.[2] They need to see you, the media, and your customers talking about your offerings everywhere and often.

THE BUYER'S JOURNEY IS NOT LINEAR

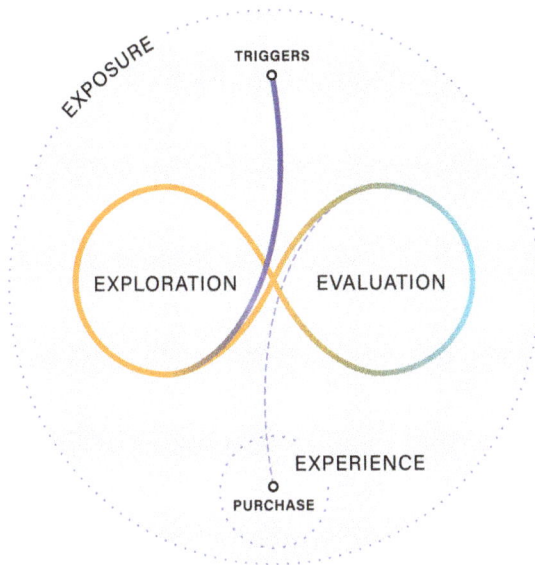

"Decoding Decisions: Making sense of the messy middle",
Google, 2020, g.co/think/messymiddle

WHY IS YOUR COMPANY STILL MARKETING LIKE IT'S 1898?

I routinely hear these golden nuggets from chief executive officers (CEOs), boards, and investors:

"I don't care if our marketing sucks. As long as our tech is badass, we're good to go."

"Our board doesn't believe in marketing. They told us to hire more salespeople, go to trade shows, and let them go hunt."

"Our sales are down, let's hack and slash the marketing budget!"

"Our product is so niche, no one will ever find it online. So why bother with digital marketing?"

"If we build it, buyers will come. Marketing is for losers who can't build stuff or write code."

"We don't need a chief marketing officer. We just need a better chief revenue officer."

I wrote this book because after three decades of being in the marketing game, I've heard enough foolishness, like the above, to fill an entire clown car. And to prove all those skeptics quoted above wrong, my agency, Clarity Quest, helped eighteen of our clients get acquired and saw one go public.

YOU NEED MARKETING LIKE YOU NEED OXYGEN; WITHOUT IT, YOU'LL SUFFOCATE IN A SEA OF COMPETITORS.

Writing this book was definitely a better option than going bald from pulling my hair out to convince you that marketing isn't a frivolous expense. In today's world of B2B tech buyers, you need marketing like you need oxygen; without it, you'll suffocate in a sea of competitors.

By investing in marketing and embracing the complexity of the modern customer journey, your tech company can position itself for long-term success or acquisition.

It's time to toss those old-fashioned marketing goggles and recognize that you're no longer living in 1898. Stop treating marketing like an outdated relic and start giving it the attention it deserves. You need to give marketing the nourishment it requires to thrive.

MY MESS-TO-SUCCESS STORY

This book is a guided tour on how health tech, IT, and biotech companies can grow through marketing. Before you take a guided tour, you should meet the tour guide.

You should know, I am a strange creature. I have both a master's degree in electrical engineering and an MBA. I currently hold eight US patents and am a member of the Forbes Agency Council.

You might say I am bilingual because I speak fluent technology and marketing.

Before I started my agency, I struggled with how to best grow health tech, IT, and biotech companies.

Rather than growth, I was eyewitness to many tech companies starving to death from a lack of marketing investments.

In total, I have a thirty-year successful track record in

marketing, business development, and product management in a wide variety of companies, from start-ups to Fortune 50 firms.

Since founding my agency, Clarity Quest, I have worked with technology and healthcare firms on marketing strategy, business planning, and marketing implementation.

The twenty-three power moves in this book are based on my journey, and my hope is to provide a road map for your success.

The stories are all true and are included to give you concrete examples. At the end of each chapter, I give you my opinions on how to apply this knowledge.

The common theme is prioritizing marketing will overcome starvation and lead to healthy growth.

Buckle up and get ready for some intriguing growth lessons that will blow your mind.

It's time to stop starving your marketing and reach your dreams. Here are twenty-three power moves you need to make.

Christine Slocumb

Stonington, CT

MOVE 1

WHY YOU MUST AVOID STARVATION MARKETING

Let's go back in time to 2008 when Anne Lodge was on a mission to help researchers create treatments and cures for some of the world's deadliest diseases.

Anne is the kind of scientist who can talk to cells and make them dance to her playlist. She has a doctorate in molecular biology, a laugh that can be heard from miles away, and enough optimism to fill a stadium.

She founded Astarte Biologics to sell characterized human cells and animal model systems to pharmaceutical companies and academia for use in research, drug discovery, and biomanufacturing.

But soon Anne found herself at a crossroads. While Astarte had some of the industry's highest-quality and best-characterized cells, it had the undeserved misfortune of having no brand visibility compared to its larger competitors.

"I was clueless about marketing, and I thought if I just listed our products on the Internet, people would find and buy them," lamented Anne.

When my agency, Clarity Quest, first engaged with her in 2014, her goal was to triple revenues.

We tried out some small Google Ads campaigns with

her tiny budget. They produced mediocre results falling short of driving revenue to meet Astarte's goals. The company needed more from marketing.

Bluntly, our agency's account director and I told her that her company was on a starvation marketing diet.

Small, random acts of marketing were not going to cut it.

Anne agreed to fund marketing at the level we recommended, spending almost as much on it as the lab and equipment. We built the best website money could buy (including the industry's first real-time, online inventory system) coupled with email marketing, LinkedIn ads targeting pharmaceutical companies, and search engine optimization (SEO) resulting in page one search engine rankings.

When we revealed the profit and loss statements (P&Ls) just three years later, the company had a compound annual growth rate of 20+ percent, investing in marketing not sales. Astarte Biologics never had a single outbound salesperson.

> BLUNTLY, OUR AGENCY'S ACCOUNT DIRECTOR AND I TOLD HER THAT HER COMPANY WAS ON A STARVATION MARKETING DIET.

In the end, Anne said: "I had to take a leap and trust in the plan. Quality marketing is expensive, but once you have the programs humming and show return on investment (ROI), it's a no-brainer to invest in it even if it's 20 percent or 30 percent of your total budget."

After a pause, Anne continued: "If I could show that

by spending $1 that I made $6, why wouldn't I continue to do it?"

In 2018, a private equity company bought and merged Astarte Biologics into a holding company. In 2020, Charles River Labs bought the holding company. Anne is now happily retired, secure in her future.

THE STARVATION MARKETING EPIDEMIC

For most tech companies, marketing is an afterthought. They don't buy into spending on marketing like Anne Lodge and Astarte did. If you are the leader of a tech company, there's a very good chance you are not spending enough on marketing.

You probably adequately invest in research, manufacturing, software development, and sales. But you haven't calculated how many leads you need to meet growth goals, so marketing gets budget table scraps.

Intentionally or unwittingly limiting marketing spend in order to fund other areas of the business may initially seem like a way to invest in product development or save money. But second-class marketing is actually killing your business.

The relegation of marketing to the proverbial *budget basement* leads to disaster. At best, your revenue will stall. At worst, you'll go out of business. I've seen it happen hundreds of times over the past thirty years, and I don't want it to happen to you.

OUR TECH IS SO INNOVATIVE, WE DON'T NEED MARKETING (AND OTHER MYTHS)

Look at an underperforming organization, and marketing underinvestment, not the product, will be the problem 90 percent of the time.

The leadership team probably thinks that marketing is just a "nice to have" or the department that creates the pretty trade show booths and sales collateral.

The truth is sales departments alone cannot generate enough leads and conversions. Consider this:

B2B buyers spend only 17 percent of the total purchase journey with sales reps.[3]

One out of four B2B buyers want to get all the necessary information about a product/service online before contacting a salesperson.[4]

More than half (53 percent) of B2B buyers say they would ideally like to buy without interacting with a salesperson.[5]

YOU CAN IMMEDIATELY SPOT A COMPANY THAT PRIORITIZES MARKETING

Find a brand you love and check out the leadership page of its website. I bet the company has a chief marketing officer, a well-rounded marketing team (or stellar agency), and a public relations partner.

When companies trust and value marketing, it shows. Your company starts to look bigger than it is and more attractive to buyers. Why wouldn't you want to join them?

WHAT ABOUT MARKETING FRAUDS?

Now you may be thinking, "What about those companies who overspend on marketing and public relations (PR) to cover up dysfunctional tech or substandard products?" One has to look no further than Theranos to find a glaring example.[6]

While these overzealous "all fluff, no tech" companies exist, I find them to be in the vast minority. Most tech companies have a quality product or service; they simply put marketing on the back burner.

MAKING THE RIGHT MARKETING MOVES
Avoid Starvation Marketing
If You Want To Grow

1. **Don't relegate marketing to the budget basement.** If you don't prioritize marketing from the outset, you'll always be playing catch-up. You have to be in front of buyers' faces all the time and that takes investment.
2. **Don't think a bigger sales team and referrals can make up for paltry marketing.** While sales and referrals may initially bring in revenues, eventually you are going to run out of "friendlies."
3. **Study a brand you personally admire.** Check out their marketing team structure and messaging. Research what they do to generate leads and build brand awareness. If you don't

know how, ask an agency with expertise doing competitive marketing program analysis.

4. **Make sure you know how you will track marketing success.** Set key performance indicators (KPIs). Invest in analytics. If you can demonstrate that $1 in marketing spend results in $5 in revenue, you can justify the budget to investors and the board all day long.

5. **Have patience.** Like good vines, marketing programs take time to bear rich fruit. Don't slash marketing budgets after only a quarter. Kill individual programs that are not working, not marketing as a whole.

MOVE 2

BETTING ONLY ON THE BEST TECH WILL LEAD TO A TRAIN WRECK

Let me share a cautionary tale. The year is 1996 and I am an engineer at a company that was #28 on the Fortune 50.

Everything was going so well.

Our product was in the pocket of every NBA star, Hollywood actor, and Wall Street executive.

But then I came to an alarming realization. When I started an MBA program while working as an engineer there, I noticed something was missing. Marketing for us was an afterthought.

"Marketing is where you go when you can't cut it as an engineer," my boss told me when I expressed interest in moving from research to marketing. I was only twenty-five and wanted my career to stay on the right track, so I remained in engineering.

Then in 1998, chinks started to appear. Our competitor invested heavily in branding, marketing, and advertising.

And six years later along comes Mr. Steve Jobs and the iPhone. And my company is sunk. We fell from a 60 percent market share to 5 percent.

If you are over forty you probably have already guessed that I worked at Motorola. If you are under forty, you're shrugging and asking, "What is Motorola?"

Oh, how the mighty have fallen. And that's the point.

Motorola is a glaring example of a company that wagered everything on its technical prowess while starving marketing. And betting only on the best tech rarely ends happily.

BETTING ON THE BEST TECH IS A LOSING PROPOSITION

Betting only on the best technology always leads to a train wreck. And I don't want it to happen to your tech company.

So I'm going to give you the way to keep your company on the rails.

The way you can stay on course is to *stop starving your marketing.*

When I ask CEOs to name companies they admire, the names that come up frequently are Nike, Tesla, and Apple.

What's the one thing all have in common? They have an unwavering commitment to marketing and brand.

While they have top-notch design and software, Apple knows they can't stake everything on their technology. Apple's marketing and brand is why people stand in line overnight for a new iPhone. Walk into an Apple Store in Paris or San Diego and you're going to have a very similar sensory experience, minus the language difference.

KEY TAKEAWAY

SUCCESS TAKES A GREAT PRODUCT OR SERVICE AND TOP-NOTCH MARKETING.

This level of marketing execution takes strategic planning, training, and significant investment.

Steve Jobs said, "Marketing is not a function. It's everything we do. It's the way we answer the phone, it's the way we greet our customers, it's the way we talk about our products, it's the way we conduct ourselves in the community. It's everything."

MAKING THE RIGHT MARKETING MOVES
Don't Just Bet On The Best Tech

1. **Don't rely only on a high-quality product or service.** Marketing and brand are the true keys to sales and valuation growth. I've seen companies with products that are merely competent with fabulous marketing have tremendous success.
2. **Start with marketing in mind.** Include a marketing plan with a resource plan, in your business plan or investment prospectus. Fund a realistic budget right out of the gate.
3. **Hold your ground when it comes to marketing budgets.** Uninformed boards and investors often recommend slashing marketing spend before anything else. If you have been tracking marketing ROI, which is imperative, show them the data and stand up for the budget.

4. **Make a Chief Marketing Officer (CMO) one of your first, not last, hires.** If you can't afford a CMO just yet, there are some great fractional CMO consultants available. Some take equity as part of compensation. Marketing agencies can also provide fractional leadership and solid strategic marketing plans if you cannot afford to hire in-house yet.

5. **Let everyone in the company know they are marketers.** Just because you don't have "marketing" in your title, doesn't mean you don't have a role to play in branding and communications. You have varied buyer personas, so you should have diverse content.

Move 3

GROWTH STALLED? GET BUSY MARKETING OR GET BUSY DYING

Mike Bogan, a pharmaceutical manufacturing veteran, started ICQ Consultants in 2007.

This down-to-business company makes sure pharmaceutical companies safely manufacture drugs and doesn't mess around when it comes to productivity and efficiency.

When the competition started to eat into his market share, Mike knew he must take action and think differently. Referrals and network connections were not enough to generate the sales pipeline he needed to meet aggressive revenue and exit goals.

Mike Bogan, and his partner Mike Gatta, leaned into marketing. ICQ hired Clarity Quest in 2019 to first build a marketing foundation and then execute all marketing as their outsourced marketing department.

We first revamped their brand messaging and positioning and created a marketing plan to get Mike and his C-level team to their revenue goals.

Then, executing as their outsourced marketing department, Clarity Quest grew the business using digital and content marketing. We tracked over $4 million in sales in one year from an omnichannel marketing program.

ICQ was successfully acquired by Ellab Corporation in 2022, realizing the Mikes' dreams. Marketing helped generate more revenue and a higher sale valuation.

ICQ CONSULTANTS' MARKETING SUCCESS METRICS

1,300+	**$4M**	
marketing-qualified pharmaceutical leads	from one-year omnichannel marketing campaign	successful acquisition in 2022

GET BUSY MARKETING OR ELSE

Many companies, like ICQ Consultants, grew on the strength of their network, friends, and referrals. These first sales to friendlies falsely cement a belief that a large marketing investment isn't necessary to grow.

But the truth is if your growth has plateaued or decreased, you should look no further than marketing. Chances are:

- Your marketing department is underfunded and under resourced.
- You haven't taken the time to develop a marketing strategic plan that is tied to business goals.
- Your sales and marketing teams don't effectively communicate with each other (or, worse, they hate and blame each other).

In the past, B2B tech companies could rely heavily on outbound sales and trade shows for lead generation. This no longer works because buying habits, especially post-pandemic, have changed.

In her book *No Forms. No Spam. No Cold Calls.*, Latané Conant shares that you need to truly understand how modern buyers buy, "Remember, modern buyers are anonymous, fragmented, and resistant. These character-istics require a vastly different approach than what we've used in the past."[7]

LOOKING TO MARKETING AS A CONVERSION GENERATOR

The average marketing department should bring in at least 35 percent of the leads that eventually convert to revenue, with sales and sales development identifying the rest. The high-performing marketing teams I've worked with identify and engage 65 percent of the leads that eventually close.

HIGH-PERFORMING
MARKETING TEAM

AVERAGE
MARKETING TEAM

Percentage of
leads marketing
departments
identify that
convert to sales.

35%

65%

Comparison of conversion percentage that can be attributed to market-ing for high-performing versus average marketing teams.

Ushering those leads from the first hand raise to sale takes time in industries, like health care, with large buying committees. Marketing nurture becomes paramount as sales teams often ignore leads that aren't ready to engage and buy immediately.

MARKETING SPEND ALLOCATION AS A PERCENTAGE OF OVERALL BUDGET

According to Deloitte's *The CMO Survey*, in 2022 marketing across all industries accounted for 12.3 percent of the overall budget and was expected to grow by 13.4 percent in 2023.[8] Deloitte concluded that B2B product companies tend to spend 10.9 percent of their budget on marketing. In comparison, B2B service companies spend 7.9 percent.

MARKETING SPEND ALLOCATION AS A PERCENTAGE OF REVENUE

According to *Gartner's 2022 CMO Spend Survey*, the healthcare industry allocated 10.1 percent of its revenue to marketing, while IT spent 10.1 percent as well. B2B service industries spent as much as 18 percent of revenue on their marketing.[9]

MAKING THE RIGHT MARKETING MOVES
Get Busy Growing

1. **Relying on sales alone leads to revenue stalls and declines.** Start-ups can often get away with a weak marketing function at first because they have penetrated such a small percentage of the marketplace. Salespeople can close the first few sales on relationships alone. But they quickly run out of "people they know."

2. **Align your sales, operations, and marketing teams.** Make sure they actually talk to one another and have shared goals. Effective pipeline generation is a team sport.

3. **Marketing a start-up into health systems and pharmaceutical companies is expensive.** My physician husband gets bombarded with emails and direct mail. A huge pile of mail is recycled every day. You're up against enterprise competitors, direct and indirect, with huge pockets. If you're a start-up launching into these markets, plan to spend at least $350,000 in year one marketing to be effective.

4. **Spend on high-return marketing, not gimmicks.** Golf outings and the sales team's travel expenses should not be charged to

marketing. Fight for this if you are a marketing leader.

5. **Generate at least 50 percent of your conversions from marketing leads.** High-performing marketing teams actually generate more conversions than the sales team. Make sure you are tracking and attributing as much as technically possible to justify the substantial investment.

Move 4

BUILDING WITH THE MARKETING TOWER OF POWER METHODOLOGY

The surest way to marketing success is building a strong foundation of brand messaging and positioning coupled with a marketing plan. Then make sure all stakeholders in the company are aligned on corporate goals, why the company exists in the first place, and its unique value propositions.

However, many companies skip these steps and move right into throwing up a website and launching lead-generation campaigns. This is like building a skyscraper on a swamp. A little wind shift comes along and the entire marketing structure collapses.

The path to marketing nirvana lies in the Marketing Tower Of Power.

CREATING THE BLUEPRINT FOR YOUR MARKETING TOWER OF POWER

Building a strong marketing foundation is the key to revenue growth. Start with a strong foundation of consistent, impactful brand messaging and positioning. Layer on quality visuals and brand identity. Stack that with a marketing plan and budget tied to business goals. These three things form your foundation: messaging, visual branding, and a marketing plan.

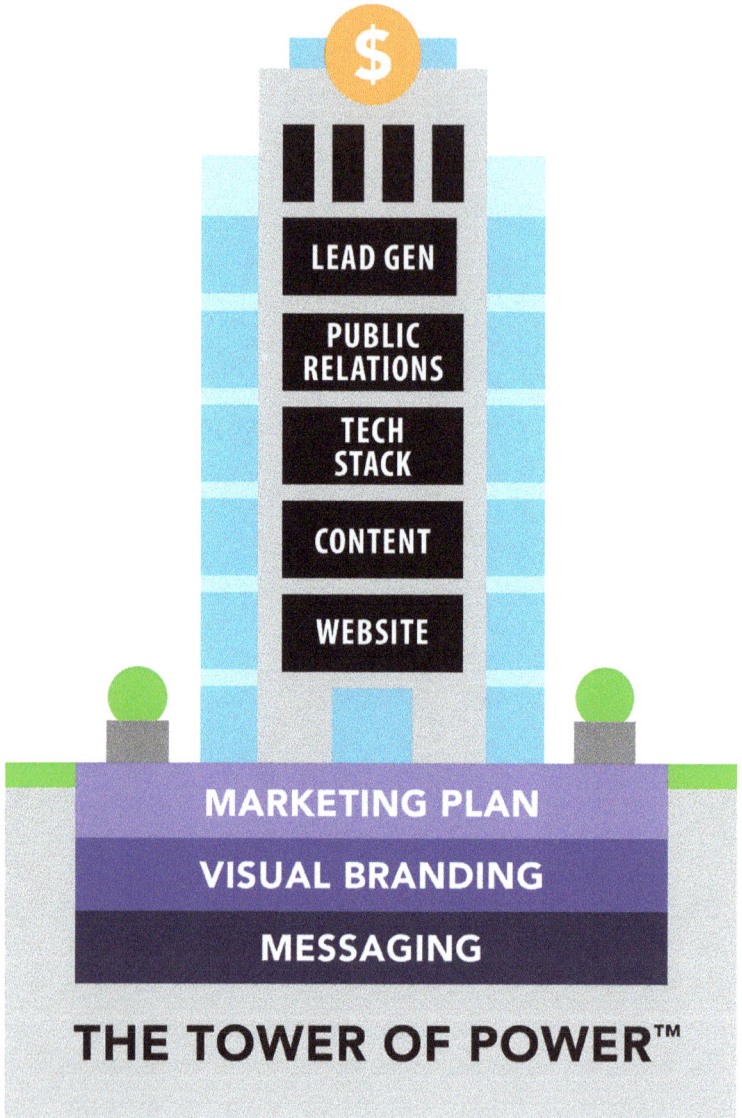

$

LEAD GEN

PUBLIC
RELATIONS

TECH
STACK

CONTENT

WEBSITE

MARKETING PLAN

VISUAL BRANDING

MESSAGING

THE TOWER OF POWER™

Top the foundation with the best search-optimized website you can afford and a killer content library. Have a plan to consistently generate new content.

Next comes your tech stack. This is where tools such as marketing automation, social media management, email list and lead data management, digital ad platforms, public relations systems, analytics tools, and audience identification come into play.

If you want to grow, you will need to take advantage of marketing technology because you simply can't do everything manually.

Finally, on the top level of the tower are public relations and lead-generation programs that take advantage of the levels below them.

MAKING THE RIGHT MARKETING MOVES
Meet The Marketing Tower Of Power

1. **Start by building a solid foundation with brand messaging and positioning.** If everyone on your team tells a different story, the marketing campaigns you build on this chaos will crumble in failure. Hash out differences of opinions and then agree on one story before you start spending money on marketing campaigns.
2. **Don't underestimate your look.** People value high-quality design. You will look larger and be able to charge a premium if your

logo, collateral, and website start from a high-quality style guide.

3. **Plan to succeed by creating a marketing strategy and budget that support your business goals.** Align your marketing to business goals. Want to exit in three years? This goal requires a different plan than a public company focused on growth and dividends.

4. **Build the best website you can afford.** Employ top-notch design, user interface, and speed. Make it easy for visitors to immediately know what you offer and how you're different.

5. **Devise a way to consistently generate quality content.** Even if you hire in-house copywriters and an agency, you'll always feel your content library is meager. Atomize every piece of content into at least ten different assets.

6. **Invest in a marketing tech stack that integrates sales systems.** Fund a marketing tech stack that is at least as advanced as your sales' customer relationship management (CRM) system. Otherwise, the sales department will force you to use their CRM for marketing campaigns, which is a recipe for disaster.

7. **Launch your lead-generation and brand awareness campaigns.** Once you have the foundation built, then you get to work on the

roof. Shout your message from the rooftops. You'll find it so much easier (and more successful) to put up those shingles if the pieces below the top floor are solid.

Move 5

YOUR BRAND CAN'T BE BLAND

I wish you could have been there the day I met Ravi Krishnan, the cofounder and general manager of Mach7 Technologies.

He faced the David vs. Goliath underdog challenge to make his small health tech company stand apart from entrenched enterprise companies like Fujifilm, Siemens, and General Electric.

He started a company that made sharing and storing immense radiological images easier, quicker, and more affordable.

Clarity Quest went to work revamping Mach7's brand messaging and positioning.

Davids cannot afford to be bland. Mach7's leadership let us run with a controversial campaign that butted heads with established norms in healthcare tech.

We gained awareness traction with a launch campaign around the tagline: "Unlock. Unleash. UnPAC." It shook up established norms in radiology image management.[10]

We took the enterprise Goliaths head-on. The new brand was bold and worked to get a small company the attention it deserved from analysts and the media.

In 2016, Mach7 beat out all its competitors in an IDC analyst report,[11] and in 2023 was featured in Best in KLAS.[12] These accolades were all a result of campaigns being built on a strong brand foundation.

Ravi says, "Years after Clarity Quest created our foundation, we still talk about how vital our branding work was to our platform taking off."

GOING FROM BLAND TO GRAND

Let's get to creating the first level of your Tower Of Power: branding, messaging, and positioning.

WHY INVEST IN BRANDING?

A strong brand will outlive your product/service offerings and increase valuation. It also makes sure everyone in the organization is working off the same playbook.

THE POWER OF A STRONG BRAND

The Power of Brand

- Conveys uniform quality, credibility, and experience
- Creates a framework for all marketing programs
- Ensures competitive differentiation
- Builds value as brands outlive products
- Ensures consistent internal and external messaging

Author Simon Sinek's philosophy that "people don't buy what you do, they buy why you do it" is one of the guiding

32

principles many companies use to start defining their brand.[13] Even in the B2B world, product benefits and features simply don't resonate with buyers the way passion does.

Bringing together a cross-section of people from various departments for an interactive storytelling workshop enables us to uncover themes that may not necessarily be visible in a person's day-to-day.

Knowing your why centers your company narrative and provides a touchstone for your brand. It breathes life and purpose into your every day and gives employees and customers a greater idea to rally around.

DEVELOP AN EFFECTIVE WHY STATEMENT

Clarity Quest's why is:

> To inspire people to reimagine and embrace marketing, so they can create an unparalleled success story.

This why informs everything the agency does, from prospecting and sales to client work. If a prospect doesn't agree with our why then they are disqualified from the pipeline because our cultures won't align.

PICK A BRAND ARCHETYPE

If everyone speaks a different language, your prospective buyers will be confused. You should identify your personality and get leadership to agree on an archetype. This will help ensure consistency of tone and voice in all communications.

THE TWELVE BRAND ARCHETYPES

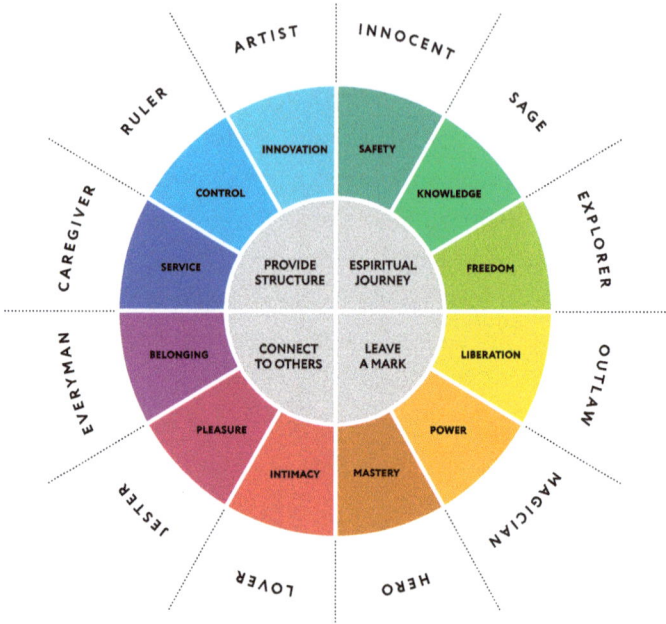

IDENTIFY THREE BRAND PROMISES OR VALUE PROPOSITIONS

Many tech companies have enough brand promises or unique value propositions to fill a crowded subway car. They want to be everything to everyone, so they end up being nothing to no one.

Pick up to three lanes and stick to them for at least a year. After that, if you get customer input to the contrary, you can change them.

And three promises are a maximum. One client asked if he could have a 1a, 1b, 2a, 2b…and my answer was a resounding "no."

BRANDED HOUSE VS. HOUSE OF BRANDS

Companies often struggle with naming and brand architecture. Should you name the product separately from the company? Should you have multiple product names or one for a platform?

WHAT'S A BRANDED HOUSE?

A branded house model prioritizes the parent brand and attaches the identity to each child brand below.

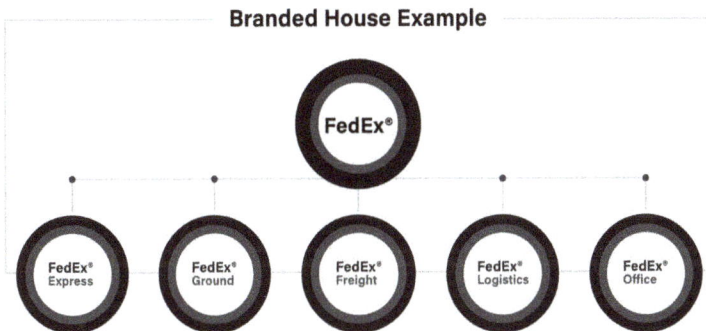

Branded House Example

FedEx®

FedEx® Express — FedEx® Ground — FedEx® Freight — FedEx® Logistics — FedEx® Office

BRANDED HOUSE PROS AND CONS

Use a branded house approach if you want your parent brand to have visibility or if funding for brand awareness is limited.

A pro for smaller companies is that by focusing all product and service branding around the parent brand and identity, you'll be able to reinforce and grow your brand value faster on a smaller budget.

A smart client and former venture capitalist, Wayne Wager, told me in my first year of running the agency, "Unless you have raised millions and plan to spend it on brand awareness, start-ups should go for simple. Go with one company and product name. Then branch out when you have more funding."

As you see with the FedEx example, if your parent brand has established value, you can leverage it by attaching it to your child brands. This strategy increases recognition for the parent brand by reaching new audiences and helps the child brands build brand value faster. A branded house also avoids brand confusion by aligning each sub-brand with the main company.[14]

BRANDER BEWARE

While a branded house can be very powerful, it can also risk the parent brand's reputation. By attaching to each child brand, your parent brand is entrusting each entity to build upon the perceived value of the overall brand, not detract from it or bring it down.

I've seen this become an issue when mergers-and-acquisitions brand integration is not done well, as it opens the door to collateral brand damage in the event of a scandal, lawsuit, or financial problem.

WHAT'S A HOUSE OF BRANDS?

"House of brands" is a branding model in which a parent company created and manages multiple individual brands under one corporate identity umbrella. Each brand has its own marketing, identity, and product offerings. The target markets and personas across the brand may differ.

Examples of house of brand models include Alphabet, Inc., General Motors, and Unilever.

House of Brands Example

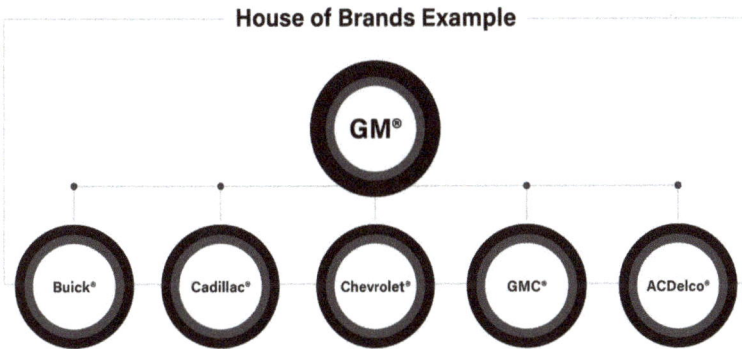

HOUSE OF BRANDS PROS AND CONS

A house of brands approach gives the ability to build distinct brand voices to serve and appeal to diverse audiences.

While your parent brand can support the child brands to an extent, each stands strong on its own and addresses unique market needs.

This brand methodology works best for large brands with diverse portfolios and deep pockets.

For most small or midsize businesses, building and supporting multiple brands is cost-prohibitive, but many fail to switch to a branded house after a merger or acquisition, and this imperils the brand.

START-UP BRANDERS BEWARE

While it can sound appealing to develop creative product branding, this approach is often not sustainable. In many cases, products or subbrands will each require brand identity creation, marketing messaging, website development, promotions, and ongoing support.

MAKING THE RIGHT MARKETING MOVES
Stand Out To Succeed

1. **Dare to be different.** Don't be scared to stand out from your competitors with controversial or thought-provoking messaging. Branding expert Sally Hogshead says: "It's good to be better but better to be different."[15]

2. **Begin with your *why*.** If everyone on the branding decision team agrees on why you exist in the first place, then everyone in the company can be a marketer and effective communicator. Buyers will also appreciate understanding your purpose for being.

3. **Don't be afraid to pick an unconventional brand archetype.** Eighty percent of tech companies pick sage because they are founded by smart people who think they have wisdom to share. But what if your customers think you're a magician or innocent? Ask them.

4. **Agree on your top three value propositions.** Not five or ten, but three main ways your brand stands out from competitors and the status quo.

5. **Choose a brand architecture.** Decide if a branded house or house of brands is a better strategy for your business. Hint: the branded house is a better choice for most small-to-midsized companies with modest budgets. Otherwise, your peanut butter will be spread too thin across your communications sandwich.

6. **Welcome doubt.** Some of the most successful branding campaigns started with media and "insiders" stating: "That idea is weird/dumb/ludicrous. Tell me more."

Move 6

WHO IS YOUR *WHO* AND WHAT IS THEIR PAIN?

Maureen Ladouceur, a former oncology nurse, understands the importance of helping big pharma get drugs to patients as soon as safely possible. She's also one of the smartest and most effective sales leaders I've ever encountered.

As the chief commercial officer of MMIT, a pharmaceutical data, analytics, and insights company, she believes patients needing lifesaving treatments shouldn't face bureaucratic roadblocks to drug access.

But she faced a monster problem.

In 2017, Maureen led MMIT's business development efforts as the VP of Sales and Go-To-Market Strategy. She and MMIT were up against an 800-pound gorilla competitor that dominated their market for years.

She and her sales team needed a way to differentiate MMIT and fast. Investors had aggressive targets for her team. She asked how Clarity Quest could help MMIT get "into the heads" of their buyers.

Clarity Quest developed a strategy to interview decision-makers in

SHE'S ALSO ONE OF THE SMARTEST AND MOST EFFECTIVE SALES LEADERS I'VE EVER ENCOUNTERED.

deals that MMIT won and lost—a "win-loss analysis." MMIT gained tremendous, often surprising, insights from the viewpoints of varied "personas," or target demographic types.

Our win-loss market research resulted in improved sales strategies that helped close enterprise pharmaceutical deals, changed product development for the better, and informed marketing content topics.

MMIT's Results From Win-Loss Analysis

Faster, improved decision-making

A more efficient sales delivery process, especially in the early stages

Increasingly effective communication

Earlier resolution of implementation concerns

New product offerings

After completing the project, Maureen commented:

"The insights we gained from win-loss analysis were critical to understanding where our clients see value and how we could be better. This reporting helped us to make better decisions that drove significant improvements to our total business performance."

MMIT grew significantly and is now part of the enterprise company, Norstella.

TURNING PAIN INTO GAIN

Before you can effectively message your solutions and launch campaigns, you need to understand your buyer personas—the demographics, likes, dislikes, and pain points of every member of your prospects' buying committee.

EVERY BUYER IS HUMAN

You need to speak directly to people motivated by emotions and rational thought, not faceless "committees" or "business entities" devoid of human desires and impulses. When creating your messaging, instead of B2B or B2C, think B4H: Business For Humans.

YOU DON'T NEED
DOZENS OF BUYER PERSONAS

You may have hundreds of thousands of individual customers, but they probably fall within three to ten personas. Don't define and target the universe. Research at least your top three personas. Think of real humans. Name them. Interview them and write quotes in their own words.

Example Of A Detailed Buyer Persona

Heather Head Nurse
CNO

Company: 200-bed hospital
Role: Buyer/Decision maker, Blocker
Education: BS, DNP, RN

When a digital vendor can prove (not promise) ROI with a strong proof-of -concept that won't drain our already depleted IT resources, I will champion the product."

Goals	Motivations	Frustrations
• Deliver high-quality, safe care	• HCAHPS scores	• Clinical team turnover
• Improve admission, discharge, and transfer efficacy	• Clinical team recognition	• Readmissions and penalties
• Reduce LOS and readmissions	• Hospital rankings	• Patient non-adherence
• Rapid, clear clinical communication	• Attract and retain top clinical talent	• Tech that doesn't lead to productivity
• Solve the staffing crisis	• Clinical productivity	

In Their Own Words

"**Simply put, my clinical team is tasked with too much.** This has been true for decades. Overpromising and underdelivering run rampant among digital health vendors. That's where I come in. My governance team (CFO, CIO, Chief of Medicine) and I thoroughly vet every viable solution based on our financial goals, operational needs, and workflow criteria. We also constantly reevaluate our existing digital health platforms to evaluate ROI. COVID and staffing shortages made tensions sky-high among clinicians. We're struggling to do right by our patients and our staff.

RATIONAL   EMOTION

EVERY HUMAN HAS AN AGENDA

A buyer may champion your system if its success will gain her a promotion. An influencer wants to appear savvy to his bosses. Some deal blockers will be afraid your latest tech may replace their job. Other blockers won't want the additional workload (infamously, IT integration departments).

It's your job to get to the heart of every person's motivations concerning your offering. And you get to those motivations by asking questions directly to members of each persona group. Or even better...having an objective third party or market research firm ask the questions and provide a report.

EMOTIONAL ROI

People hate pain. Solving a nagging issue at work that deprives someone of sleep or costs an owner money motivates a person like nothing else. Large tech purchases can make or break careers.

You better be able to convey the "emotional ROI," along with the measurable financial ROI, of your solution to each human on the buying committee.

Here are some examples:

- **A system that gives Kim, the HR director,** an improved employee retention number leading to fewer complaints from the C-suite.

- **Software that improves collections so Ken, the chief financial officer (CFO),** can meet his annual margin target and sleep well at night.

- **A workflow that helps Mary, EVP of patient safety** in a large health system, to improve patient safety scores leading to a long sought after promotion to the C-suite.

If you are just a "nice to have" you're not going to stand out. Your message will be lost in a crowded world.

(For further study, I recommend the article "What CMOs Need To Know About Buyer Personas." Learn how CMOs can utilize buyer personas correctly. Josh Steimle highlights common mistakes companies make when using buyer personas and provides recommendations for proper use.[16])

MAKE THE RIGHT
MARKETING MOVES
Find Your Who And Name Their Pain

1. **List your main personas:** economic buyers, influencers, advocates, and potential deal blockers. Give them each a name and develop a profile for each like the examples above.

2. **Define the "emotional ROI"** of your product. Solve at least one pain point for economic buyers, show influencers how you can make them look smart, and remove at least one hurdle for blockers.

3. **Tell each persona on the buying committee how you are different.** Why should he buy from you? Differentiate yourself from the competition—in his language. Develop content in formats attractive to how each persona likes to consume information.

4. **Gather the LinkedIn profiles of at least twenty-five actual buyers.** See what they have in common: which groups they belong to, who they read and follow. If you're a startup with no customers, pick out twenty-five potential targets.

5. **Make your buyer the hero.** She's taking a risk on you. Show there's a potentially huge payoff for her in the form of fame or fortune after the sale.

Move 7

WHAT'S YOUR COMPANY'S AWARD SPEECH?

In 2019 Carol Kingsley was faced with the challenge of re-branding a print communications company into a health-care tech company.

As the new VP of sales and marketing at Previon, Carol was at a crossroads.

As Previon migrated from compliance communications to the healthcare technology space, Carol wanted memorable messaging that would immediately resonate with the company's new target audience and differentiate them in the market.

But it was not just Carol's call to make. Twelve people wanted a say in the overhaul including the CEO, CFO, and chief technical officer (CTO). Each had diverging ideas.

Clarity Quest ran a brand messaging session. We were lucky enough to do this right before the pandemic, so we broke the meeting attendees into teams and ran this exercise. Each team had to write the acceptance speech for a "Best in Health Tech Industry Award."

The speeches were informative, engaging, and most importantly, different. In the end, we took messaging elements from all three groups, which helped us develop an impactful and memorable tagline:

HEALTH AWARE. CARE EMPOWERED.

The new tagline and brand messaging helped Previon launch into an entirely new space and be seen as leaders in preventative care communications and at-home self-collection health screening test kit fulfillment.

AND THE AWARD GOES TO...

Whether it's social media, email, or another digital channel, your potential customers are bombarded with messages at every turn. To stand out from the competition, you must tell a clear, compelling story that cuts through the noise and makes your potential customers take notice.

> ## MARKETING IS NO LONGER ABOUT THE STUFF THAT YOU MAKE, BUT ABOUT THE STORIES YOU TELL.
> Seth Godin, author and entrepreneur

B2B start-ups often skip the brand positioning step and go headfirst into creating a website and executing digital campaigns. This method often fails. You're missing the chance to emotionally connect with customers using a compelling origin story or impactful mission.

In ZAG, Marty Neumeier recommends writing your company's obituary.[17] I've created a more positive spin on this exercise: writing your company's industry award speech.

When you don't take the time to develop brand messaging, marketing, sales, your board, and your C-suite will have different opinions about how to talk about your company and its products and solutions. There will be no brand cohesion.

This exercise is a fun and robust way to get everyone to align. It's also a great alternative when teams get stuck on their why.

MAKING THE RIGHT MARKETING MOVES
Write Your Company's Award Acceptance Speech

1. **Use creative brainstorming to get to your company's *why* and value propositions.** You can run a simple exercise with your team to craft bold positioning called "write your company's award acceptance speech."

2. **Create a list of stakeholders to participate in the workshop.** The ideal participant number for this exercise is eight to twelve. If a person is going to have a say in your messaging decisions (e.g., board member), invite them to this exercise.

3. **Break into teams of no more than four people per group.** Any larger and someone's voice will be left out.

4. **Ask each group to write down an award acceptance speech.** Ask them to highlight

how the company has affected or will affect society, the industry, and their community.

5. **Give the speeches.** Have one person from each group give the speech out loud and record it, if possible. You can get quick transcriptions from Zoom or Rev.com.

6. **Make the speech sundae.** Take the best bits from each speech to form vision and mission statements. Save more tactical ideas in a virtual parking lot.

7. **Get approval on the finalized speech from all important stakeholders.** Get approval now from the C-level and the board of directors. Distribute to the entire team.

    I've facilitated this exercise with many groups. It's fun, illuminating, and most importantly, it works to break even the staunchest introvert out of her shell.

Move 8

FEATURES AND BENEFITS DON'T SELL HEARTS AND MINDS

"Are hospitals the next Blockbuster Video?"

That was a headline that struck fear to healthcare executives.

Here is the backstory. The year was 2022, and Chief Strategy Officer Cynthia Church and Marketing Manager Amy Oliver led the marketing department at the health tech company Xealth. The pair faced a huge dilemma.

Xealth's technology platform makes health systems more financially stable with better patient engagement and outcomes.

But Xealth's target personas are C-level leaders, who are notoriously hard to reach via traditional marketing campaigns. And they are even harder to engage with given losses and ugly balance sheets post-COVID-19. They don't want to spend on new systems unless absolutely necessary.

But Church and Oliver needed to get their value proposition out to C-level leaders in health systems and get them to engage.

My agency knew it would take some emotion-stirring, creative content to connect with these leaders and cut through the clutter. As Ann Handley writes in *Everybody Writes*, "B2B is more emotional, not less (than B2C). The stakes are higher: a job on the line, a reputation at risk."[18]

The Clarity Quest team sifted through Xealth's content and saw their CEO Mike McSherry had written a poem. It was an unconventional asset, but we thought it would resonate with Xealth's target audience.

The content asset we developed focused on the increasingly competitive environment in which large health systems operate by drawing an analogy to the demise of Blockbuster Video. Like the entertainment industry, health care is evolving rapidly, and technology is changing consumer and patient behavior and expectations. Health systems must adapt or perish.

To generate top-of-funnel leads with this valuable content, the content team leaned into the Xealth CEO's personality and penchant for penning limericks on his personal social feeds. In addition, our agile digital team honed in on Xealth's list of 150+ dream clients for an account-based marketing approach targeting specific health systems.

The Xealth ad is a great example of the Von Restoroff Effect, which predicts that when multiple homogeneous stimuli are presented, the stimulus that differs from the rest is more likely to be remembered.[19] Health system leaders are not used to seeing an old VHS tape in their LinkedIn feeds. And they are not used to seeing fear as a stimulus. So the ad stood out.

The aftermath? The first campaign generated fifty-plus engagements in the first weeks, including tens of top-of-funnel C-level prospects.

Xealth's LinkedIn Ad circa 2022, used with permission.

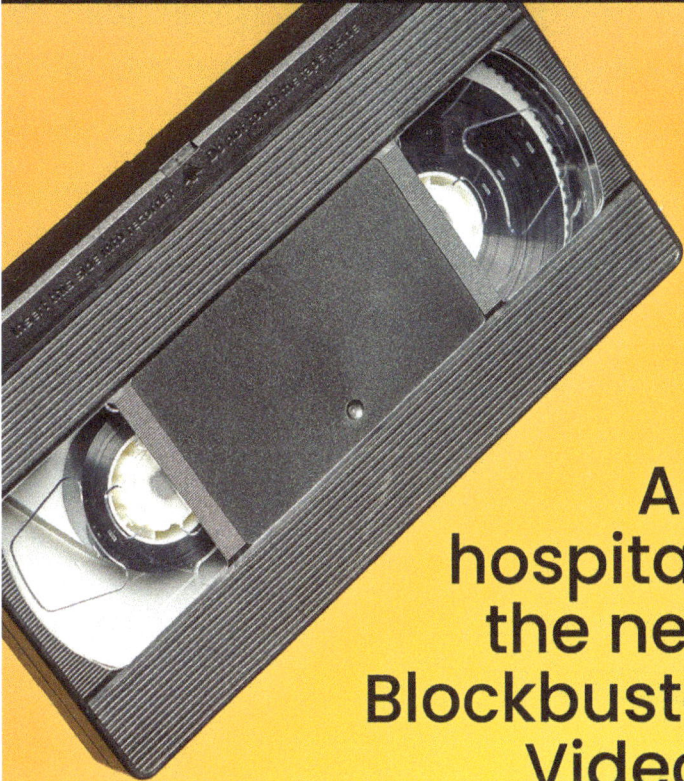

Xealth
6,281 followers
Promoted

Are hospitals the next Blockbuster Video? Patients want competence and convenience. If your health system doesn't provide it, your competition will.

Are
hospitals
the next
Blockbuster
Video?

10 Digital Health Strategy Must-Haves.
xealth.com

FORGET FEATURES AND BENEFITS

Behavioral science shows even highly technical buyers purchase based on emotional cues.

When I went to buy my first new car, I did a ton of research and had a list of all the features I liked at the price range I could afford. I went to the dealer 95 percent sure I wanted a Subaru Outback to traverse the backroads of Arizona, while still being practical on Phoenix roads. Then I walked onto the showroom floor.

A gleaming, big red Isuzu Rodeo SUV called my name. It was bigger than I wanted with awful gas mileage, but I immediately envisioned how I'd look sitting high up in the driver's seat on Arizona's rugged off-road trails. I was sold and walked out with the Rodeo. My engineering-trained brain and logic went out the window.

Companies, even highly technical B2B firms, must develop messaging that connects emotionally with their prospects. Emotion drives 80 percent of decision-making. Data drives the remaining 20 percent.

But leadership, legal departments, and regulatory reviewers often kill content ideas that focus on emotion, humor, or storytelling. They want to play it "safe" and not offend anyone. The result is sterile content that doesn't connect or convert, but only takes up space.

"Don't be afraid to give your writing a distinctive, conversational 'voice.' It shouldn't sound like a term paper," says Julie Wolk, the chief marketing officer at innovative health tech company Carium. "Great messaging informs, provokes, entertains, and/or inspires."

Make sure your content isn't putting people to sleep. Go beyond traditional facts and figures with your content. Buyers, even really intelligent ones, make purchases on emotion even if they don't realize it.

MAKING THE RIGHT MARKETING MOVES
Seven Ways To Incorporate Emotion Into Your Marketing Messaging

1. **Begin at the beginning.** Share a story of why you started the business or created the product. Simon Sinek, in his groundbreaking Starting With Why, popularized the notion of figuring out your why and then how you're different and what you do. Origin stories interest people.

2. **Incorporate humor.** Satire and fun can be used in good taste, even in sensitive situations and industries, like health care. My agency had a healthcare software client that gave humorous awards to medical practices' billing employees who normally don't get any love or recognition working from the basement or back offices. They loved the awards, which lightened the tedium of their daily routines.

3. **Use fear.** Buyers worry about missing out or getting bested by a competitor. My agency used a demographic targeting technique in which we contacted every health system in

a sixty-mile radius of a health system that had bought our client's software. When the large marquee hospital saw its tiny competitor had something it didn't to reduce patient leakage, they were immediately interested to learn more.

4. **Tell a story from a user's perspective.** "Day in the life" stories are very effective. Create an illustrated "before and after" collateral piece or video that shows how you improve the end users' experiences. For example, they may finish their day exhausted and frustrated before using your product but satisfied and calm once they use it. My agency successfully used easy-to-digest infographics showing nurses how a new workflow tool could make their jobs easier.

5. **Take a lesson from Hollywood.** Tell the story of how your product slays a big metaphorical monster or turns an underdog into a hero. Everyone loves a come-from-behind story.

6. **Communicate data in an unexpected way.** Highly technical buyers do respond to facts, but be sure not to bore them. Instead of a simple ROI calculator, consider an interactive online experience that gives users personalized use cases along with typical savings and efficiency data. Without a story, your messaging

looks like a pile of data. Data alone does not move the needle to conversion.

7. **Tap into an unexpected sense.** Have you ever smelled an apple pie that triggered a long-forgotten memory? While marketing content often triggers visual and auditory senses, consider how to incorporate taste or smell.

Move 9

FAILING TO CREATE A STRATEGIC MARKETING PLAN IS PLANNING TO FAIL

April Wilson had a nagging issue. She served as the vice president of analytics and marketing for a midmarket, private-equity-backed company and had a puzzlement on her hands.

Her company had the undeserved reputation for being "just a billing statement print shop" when they had, in fact, developed patent-pending intelligent revenue cycle technology for health care.

April knew she needed the healthcare industry to sit up and take notice of her company as a valued partner for all aspects of the patient financial experience, and not just as a billing statement vendor.

The company had acquired four smaller companies. But sales and marketing in the five entities were operating independently. Investors and leadership wanted a consolidated marketing strategy to drive the sales pipeline across all the business units.

That's when April invited my agency to help solve the puzzle with a strategic marketing plan.

"I had a big mountain to climb in transforming the marketing strategy, and I needed a great agency sherpa to get it done," said April. "It was crucial to find an agency partner who was data-driven, agile, and comfortable telling us if any aspects of our rebranding strategy were stupid. Yes, I said stupid. I didn't want a 'yes, dear' partner—I needed a fellow warrior in the trenches to rework the strategy, and that's what brought me to Clarity Quest."

Together we got to work creating a new plan centered on getting online traction and the attention of analysts. Their target buyer was impossible to reach at trade shows and never opened their emails.

We needed our target audience to read about what we were doing in trade magazines or see us mentioned in a Gartner report.

The media and analyst blitz, combined with a robust digital strategy and a thought-leadership book by the president, drove a 250 percent increase in sales meetings and a bookings increase of 120 percent year-over-year.

Marketing went from being a sales support organization to a department capable of driving the business in its own right, all thanks to a revamped go-to-market strategy.

NOTHING LESS THAN A STRATEGIC MARKETING PLAN WILL DO

Marketing leaders at high-growth companies say their two most important success factors are the communication and documentation of a clear strategy, followed by the commitment to that strategy.

While many MBA programs teach marketing plans, a surprising number of companies don't take the time to generate them. It's astounding how many midmarket companies with thousands of employees slap together a budget spreadsheet and call it their "plan."

Yet, the C-level and boards are holding marketing leaders more accountable to actual KPIs, objectives and key results (OKRs), and revenue metrics than they did in the past. According to *The CMO Survey*, 58 percent of marketing leaders say they face increased pressure from CEOs and 45 percent from CFOs to prove the effectiveness of their efforts.[20]

Ernest Wassmann, a former CEO who is now a business advisor, said: "A good strategy and tactics will equal growth, but a bad strategy and tactics will equal death."[21]

Be warned: a bad strategy and great tactics means you will die faster.

How can you expect to reach your goal destination without a road map? Marketing strategies, analytics, and tech stacks become more complex every year. Leaders face a dizzying number of challenges and opportunities to manage at warp speed than they did just a few years ago.

Marketing teams can only succeed with a strategic plan that maps to business goals.

NO MORE RANDOM ACTS OF MARKETING

When clients ask my agency to create a plan and then they buy into it and its execution, they are far more successful in growing revenues and valuations than their peers who launch ad hoc marketing campaigns.

I don't see many companies with an approved plan making wasteful advertising and trade show investments.

A marketing plan serves the following functions:

- It shows how marketing will support business goals.
- It tracks costs and measures ROI.
- It fosters conscious budget trade-offs such as whether you should invest in public relations or digital advertising if you only have the funds for one.
- It identifies resource gaps and helps solidify hiring timelines.
- It captures thinking and assumptions. Do you remember why you nixed analyst relations or started pay-per-click display ads three years ago? I bet no. And what happens when your marketing leader leaves, and all the marketing plans only lived in her head?
- It serves as a template for future years' plans. Trust me on this one. Once you make the initial investment, you'll be excited about how easy it is to create future plans and budgets.

Benefits Of A Well-Crafted Marketing Plan

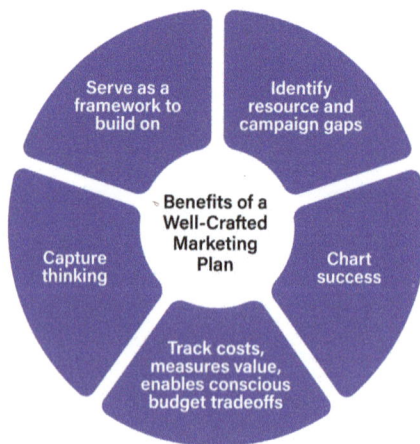

STRATEGIC FRAMEWORKS FOR MARKETING PLANS

Use a "Goal POST" framework. Developed by Clarity Quest, POST stands for Performance, Objectives, Strategies, and Tactics. Using this framework, you align corporate business goals to the marketing function.

Goal POST Marketing Plan Framework

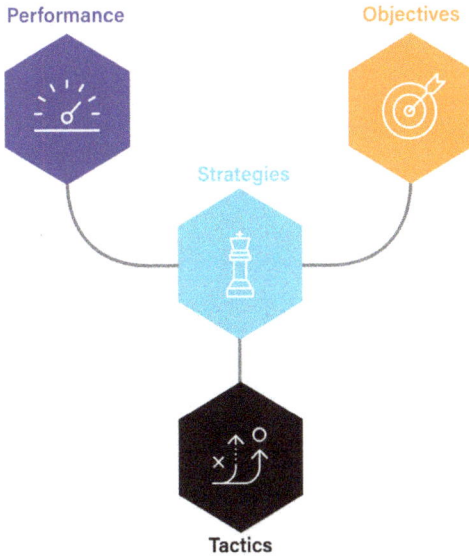

Performance identifies what success looks like and how you will measure it.

Objectives are corporate KPIs such as revenue targets or exit strategies.

Strategies are marketing strategies that will support each corporate objective.

Tactics are individual campaigns that support one or more marketing strategies.

I also like the V2MOM method developed by Marc Benioff that's used at Salesforce. V2MOM stands for:

- Vision
- Values
- Methods
- Obstacles
- Measures

ELEMENTS TO INCLUDE IN EVERY MARKETING PLAN

After getting the high-level Goal POST or V2MOM defined, it's time for the detailed marketing plan. Here are elements to consider including in your plan:

Business goals. Stating the business goals up front sets the stage for a marketing plan that's aligned with your company's high-level objectives.

Business goals answer these overarching questions that affect the business:

- Do you want to get acquired in a certain number of years?
- What are your short-term and long-term growth goals expressed as revenue and EBITDA?[22]
- Are there new verticals or products on the horizon?

Performance definition. How will you define marketing success when you look back in six months or a year? Develop and agree upon marketing KPIs that truly affect your business.

Challenges to solve and solutions. Define the challenges you're currently facing and how this marketing plan will help overcome these hurdles, such as new competitors, long sales cycles, or a lack of brand awareness.

Situational Analysis. A staple of every MBA program is the strengths, weaknesses, opportunities, and threats (SWOT) matrix, which lets companies see a situational overview at a glance.

Competitive analysis. Start by listing your direct and indirect competitors.

Direct competitors offer very similar products and services to your target audiences.

Companies usually know who their direct competitors are. If not, ask your sales managers who are on the front lines talking to prospects every day—they should be able to rattle off a list.

Indirect competitors offer similar products or services or target a slightly different audience. For example, you are selling software to urgent care companies and your indirect competitors are selling software with the same features to long-term care organizations.

Note that sticking with the status quo or in-house development can also be your competitors, especially when it comes to software.

Many companies think they have a unique offering, but after digging deeper, they usually find they have multiple indirect competitors. It's not unusual during market research to find that your prospects actually think an indirect competitor does exactly what you do.

Determine your target market focus and size. Successful marketing requires focus and discipline. Initially, start-ups often cast a wide net and target everyone to keep the lights on and their angel investors happy. Yet over time, this haphazard approach will stall sales.

Buyers expect to see themselves in your content and messaging. This requires a significant amount of personalization. If you try to chase more than three audiences, you're going to burn out your marketing department and spread your marketing budget so thin that you won't meet your objectives.

A logical first step in selecting target markets is determining how many top-of-funnel leads are needed to support your conversion goals. To your surprise, your market size may not be large enough to support your revenue goals.

Pricing. Although it's one of the classic four Ps of marketing,[23] marketing is often taken out of pricing discussions by turning the exercise over to sales and product managers.

This is a mistake because marketing is the one department that knows how price affects how customers view your brand. If you communicate a premium brand message via your content and website but your value proposition is your affordable price, this disconnect will only confuse your customers. Your brand messaging and positioning need to align with your pricing structure.

Marketing tactics (programs and campaigns). Prioritize your channels, define execution sequences, and tie them to the above strategies and KPIs.

Ownership and timelines. To stay on track with your marketing plan, it's important to determine who does what and when. Build out assignments monthly and identify specific people, not departments, when doling out responsibilities.

MAKING THE RIGHT MARKETING MOVES
No More Random Acts Of Marketing

1. **Take the time to create a well-crafted *strategic* marketing plan.** A budget is not a plan. A bundle of tactics is not a plan. Creating your company's first truly strategic marketing plan mapped to business goals is a significant investment in time, resources, and budget. However, it will pay dividends in revenue growth and productivity for years.

2. **Embrace your inner planner.** Even if you've only ever run tactical campaigns, I promise there's a strategic planner in you. Think of the last time you scheduled a vacation, mapped out a running route, or juggled your kids' schedules. You can do it!

3. **Trust in the plan.** Every one of our clients that took the time to craft a plan with us and then execute it has succeeded in meeting their growth or exit goals. Eighteen of my agency's clients have been acquired and one went public. All had a marketing plan.

4. **See efficiencies after generating the first plan.** The first plan will be the most difficult to create. You'll be able to create next year's plan in half the time of the first, and if you leave, your company will have a blueprint that outlives your tenure.

5. **Conduct a marketing competitive analysis.** A lot of companies understand their competitors' offerings; fewer know their competitors' marketing programs and approximate budget. There are lots of deciphering tools available to help you figure this out. They are worth the investment, especially in the online marketing arena.

Move 10

Cori Omundson, currently the CEO and founder of Rising Wines Collective, was a marketing strategist and account director at Clarity Quest for four years. She was excellent at getting CEOs to invest in marketing.

She recalls sitting down with Anne Lodge, the CEO of Astarte Biologics, and telling her the good and bad news. "We can get you where you want to go. But it's not going to be cheap; it is an investment. Marketing isn't just one tactic; it's the sum of programs together that gets results."

Anne approved a fivefold increase in marketing spend after Cori shared our agency's recommendations.

When I asked the secret to her success in getting C-levels to invest more in marketing, Cori recounted, "I am passionate about what's in the client's best interest, and it's about optimization through continued analysis. We pivot as needed, cutting what doesn't work and rationalizing additional spending to ensure we maximize their ROI. It's about building trust and making informed decisions."

Cori is now successfully putting her skills at convincing others to invest by getting angel funding for her own venture.

PLEASE DON'T LAND HERE FIRST

If you like to read books out of sequence, you probably landed here first. The number one complaint I hear from marketing leaders is "I can't get my [insert C-level title] to approve the budget I need to get the results she wants."

If your boss is narrow-minded about the power of marketing, show him this book. But if you're a marketing leader that simply takes last year's marketing spend and adds 30 to 50 percent expecting the CFO will cut it back, you need to look in the mirror.

MARKETING INTO HEALTH SYSTEMS AND PHARMA TAKES MOOLAH

Plan to spend at least 8 percent of your incremental revenue target on marketing. By incremental revenue, I mean your sales target above and beyond what you can achieve without marketing. You can spend slightly less if you are in a super niche market without many competitors (but I haven't seen that scenario often).

Figuring out how much is enough—or too much—and where to spend your money can be daunting.

To come up with a marketing budget, you need to consider various factors, including your business goals, your industry, how much your competitors spend, and your company's revenue and growth goals.

Leadership's Marketing Expectations vs. The Budget and Expected ROI

| Marketing
Plan | Marketing
Budget | **Expected
ROI** |

Based on an original concept by Chris Branch and Hugo Suissas

HOW TO DEVELOP YOUR BUDGET

Calculate, don't copy. Many marketing leaders whip out the previous year's budget and add 30 percent. Then, they go back and forth with the CFO and CEO to justify spending. This is lazy marketing and won't get the budget you need or the results you want.

Position your budget like your brand. When presenting your marketing budget to senior leaders, position it as an investment, not a cost center. If you expect them to invest, you must be aligned with the corporate goals and show how you will measure marketing success regarding revenue.

Align marketing objectives to business goals. Before creating a budget, use your Goal POST exercise to align business goals to marketing by defining performance measurements, objectives, strategies, and tactics. This way your executive team can clearly see how marketing strategies and tactics support high-level business objectives.

LET'S GET CALCULATING

There is no one correct way to calculate a budget, but here are five popular methods.

Method #1. Percentage Of Projected Revenue

Forecast your revenue goal for the coming year and allocate a percentage of the total gross revenue for marketing campaigns. That's easy. The difficult part is figuring out the percentage to use.

For comparison, here's data on marketing as a percentage of revenue by annual revenue and employee headcount.

Marketing Budget as Percentage of Revenue

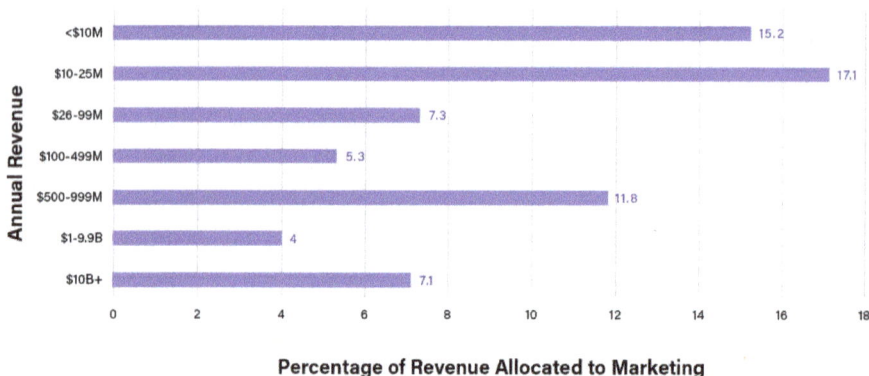

Annual Revenue	Percentage of Revenue Allocated to Marketing
<$10M	15.2
$10-25M	17.1
$26-99M	7.3
$100-499M	5.3
$500-999M	11.8
$1-9.9B	4
$10B+	7.1

Percentage of Revenue Allocated to Marketing

Marketing Budget By Industry

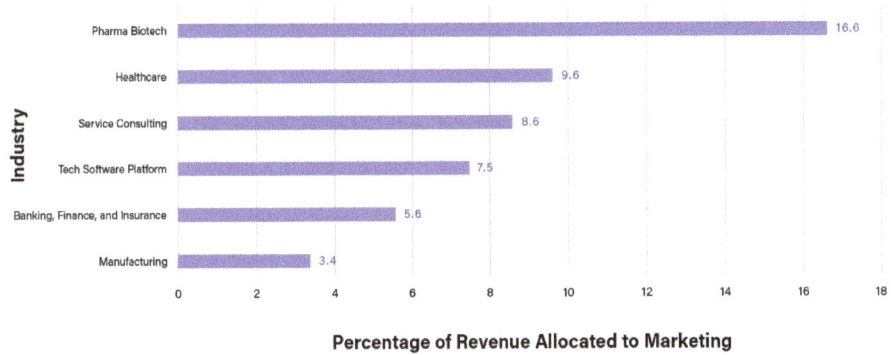

Percentage of Revenue Allocated to Marketing

Source: "The CMO's Guide To Setting And Defending Your Marketing Budget And ROI."[24]

Method #2. Percentage Of Net Sales

Calculate the same way as method #1, except deduct returns, discounts, and allowance from revenue.

Method #3. Percentage Of Budget

For this method you'll need to work closely with your CFO because you'll need to know the entire company's budget. This can be one of the trickiest (and slowest) methods because you are dependent on every other department in the company.

	% Budget	% Revenue
B2B Product	10.9%	8.5%
B2B Services	7.9%	10.3%
B2C Product	17.8%	16.1%
B2C Services	10.9%	10.0%

Source: The CMO Survey.[25]

Method #4. Percentage Of Growth Delta

If your current annual revenue is $2 million and you want to get to $5 million, then your growth delta is $3 million. To determine marketing spend, multiply your growth delta anywhere from 10 percent for niche-market B2B to 30 percent for software-as-a-service (SaaS).

The thinking behind this method is you can probably generate the current revenue in the future with the same marketing budget. But if you want to grow revenue, you need more marketing investment.

Method #5. Desired Conversions Or New Customers

This method requires that you know your cost of acquiring new customers, which is an important metric you should calculate even if you don't use this process. Some companies include only marketing costs in the cost of acquisition, and some combine sales plus marketing costs.

The formula: total closes x acquisition cost = marketing budget.

SHOULD I GENERATE MONTHLY, QUARTERLY, OR ANNUAL BUDGETS?

While it's OK to map out KPIs or goals quarterly, I like detailed monthly marketing budgets. Quarterly campaigns slip too easily. It's more work to map out monthly, but it's less overwhelming when you see what has to be done in bite-sized chunks.

RIGHTSIZE, DON'T GORGE

While the vast majority of companies spend too little on marketing, some B2B tech companies go crazy after an initial cash infusion, throwing lavish user group parties or mailing $1,000 logo products to prospects.

Skip the caviar, two-tier trade show booths, and yacht parties. Don't bury expenses like golf outings and sporting event tickets in the marketing budget. Spend first on proven digital marketing, concierge suites, and public relations campaigns.

MAKING THE RIGHT MARKETING MOVES
Get A Bigger Budget From Your Board Or Investors

One of my first bosses told me, "In God I trust. Everyone else, bring data." He was repeating a quote often attributed to Professor Edward Deming. The point is hard facts are hard to dispute and get you more investment dollars.

1. **Focus on results tied to business, not activities.** Your marketing team may be "hard at work" on XYZ, but the tactics don't make the investment profitable. What goal(s) did they accomplish that support business goals such as revenue growth or a valuation boost?

Results (Good)	Activities (Nobody Cares)
Increased conversions from first-touch marketing from 35 percent to 50 percent.	Increased click-through rates by 25 percent.
SEO rankings contributed $5 million to revenue.	Had 4,000 website form completions.
Two target prospects saw our cover story in XYZ Magazine and they converted to paying customers.	Placed 10 articles in trade journals.

2. **Show the relationship of results to goals.** Stats in a vacuum are useless. Set specific goals and track against them.

Results (Good)	Results (Great)
Increased conversions from first-touch marketing from 35 percent to 50 percent.	Increased conversions from first-touch marketing 50 percent vs. a goal of 40 percent.
SEO rankings contributed $5 million to revenue.	SEO rankings contributed to $5 million in revenue vs. a KPI of $4.5 million.
Five target prospects saw our cover story in trade journals, and they converted to paying customers.	Converted five prospects added to the funnel from first-touch PR campaigns compared to a goal of four.

3. **Overcommunicate and be consistent with your reporting format.** Find out the communication format your approval audience likes. Do they want PowerPoint and statistics, or do they respond better to a bulleted list? Either way, be consistent and don't change when budget approval time rolls around.

4. **Tell the truth. The *whole* truth.**

   Marketing: Our new mobile campaign brought in $1 million in revenue.

   Board: How much of our spend does the campaign represent?

   Marketing: 8 percent.

   Board: What happened with the other 92 percent of our budget?

   Marketing: *crickets*

   Have an answer and a corrective action plan when you're falling short. Any concealment or lack of transparency will hurt your

cause. Honesty is always the best policy—
no exceptions.

5. **Use an authoritative (not arrogant) tone.**
    Investors can smell fear from a mile away. Be
    prepared, practice, and confidently present
    what you believe in.

Move 11

BUILD A DIGITAL MANSION, NOT AN ONLINE SHACK

In 2006, Dave Morin and Jim Price led a health tech spinoff out of the University of Michigan. Cielo MedSolutions' patient registry system performed a critical health service: it helped track the data of marginalized communities to increase immunization rates and lower pediatric lead exposure, among other things.

Cielo had fewer than twenty employees and a couple of angel investors. So, the budget was tight. But Dave and Jim always found funding for marketing.

We built the best website that their budget would allow. And I was early to the SEO game and convinced Dave to let me structure their site and write their web copy to rank highly in Google search results pages.

A few years later, Cielo was successfully acquired by Advisory Board.

How did Advisory Board find Cielo when looking for acquisition targets? A high ranking on a Google search results page was part of the equation.

I OWE MY AGENCY'S SUCCESS TO THREE THINGS: LOYAL TEAM MEMBERS, HARD WORK, AND A KICK-ASS WEBSITE.

YOUR WEBSITE IS YOUR MARKETING HOME

I owe my agency's success to three things: loyal team members, hard work, and a kick-ass website.

In running the agency, I always spend as much time and money as I can on website design, development, and SEO. And it has paid dividends. When we were only four people, the website looked like we were twenty, and when we were fifteen we looked like fifty.

Our sales team has high conversion rates selling Clarity Quest's marketing services because the website is the best business development rep and never complains. Our website brings us leads that are 80 percent down the buying journey.

A quality website is a lead generator, a validator, and a communication vehicle. Every one of your marketing and public relations programs will depend heavily on it. Don't cut corners and don't skimp on a cheap site that won't scale and isn't optimized to show up in online searches.

GET FOUND WITH SEO

A website that's not optimized for search is like building a shack on the most gorgeous beachfront lot.

Whenever a CEO insists SEO is not important because no one will ever search for his product online, I bet him a lunch. In twenty-two years, I've never lost.

In May 2023, there were over nine billion Google search queries every day.[26]

If someone isn't looking for your product category, your service offering, or, indirectly, the pain you can solve, then you don't have a feasible business.

SEO as a topic could take an entire book, but I can highly recommend the content on MOZ.com to start your education on the subject.

IF SOMEONE ISN'T LOOKING FOR YOUR PRODUCT CATEGORY, YOUR SERVICE OFFERING, OR, INDIRECTLY, THE PAIN YOU CAN SOLVE, THEN YOU DON'T HAVE A FEASIBLE BUSINESS.

Design your site to rank highly in search results pages. Even if you don't want to rank today, there will be a day in the future when it's critical.

MAKING THE RIGHT MARKETING MOVES
Treat Your Website With The Honor It Deserves

1. **Start with a website requirements document.** Getting your requirements down on paper will ensure your website supports business goals and technical needs.

2. **Build a site map.** A clear and organized visual structure of your site will allow you to see how visitors will navigate your pages and will make sure you are covering all topic areas. It will also help your developers

make the right user interface and structural decisions.

3. **Finish brand messaging and SEO research before writing web copy.** The best web copy is the perfect combination of art and science: creative visuals, sexy headlines, and search engine optimization. Make sure you're walking the balance beam and not straying too far in any one direction.

4. **Wireframe complex pages.** Wireframes are visual outlines that help designers and developers understand the desired content and functionality of each page and ensure that everyone is in agreement before starting to build the actual website. They can be simple hand-drawn sketches or more sophisticated digital prototypes.

5. **Create at least two designs.** Some of our agency's best web design work has come from combining a "little bit of design A" with a "dash of design B." Create a homepage and subpage in at least two different formats or themes.

6. **Test on all platforms before launch.** Make sure you view and test your website on all the major browsers and mobile platforms. Include devices of different sizes and brands in your testing.

7. **Update often.** Your website is a living asset. Don't launch it and forget it. Put together a plan to regularly add new content and execute on that plan.

Move 12

CONTENT IS THE ENTIRE BACK ROW OF THE CHESSBOARD

SONIFI Health's Krista Gellert, marketing director, and Meghan Seus, vice president of product marketing, approached Clarity Quest with a content challenge.

SONIFI's patient experience platform provides interactive technology for TV, door signage, in-room whiteboards, mobile, and other digital communication tools that reduce nurse burnout and better educate and entertain patients and their families.

SONIFI had an age-old issue: their content sounded like everyone else. They were being seen as a commodity in the market. They needed to stand out.

We did a competitive messaging analysis that looked at all content offerings. All the competitive content was boring, conservative, and overly used "hospital-speak."

We reframed the content strategy, focusing on a day in the life of nurses and the patient's voice to reach target personas. Our content focused on being fun and inviting information such as what life would be like without those dirty hospital room whiteboards and how the most-watched Netflix movies in hospitals affect patient education videos.

SONIFI's new content strategy highlighted that a hospital stay doesn't have to lack hospitality.

This new content strategy, go-to-market plan, and calendar will help them shine in a crowded digital communication field. SONIFI now has a plan that shows they are modernizing the patient experience to reduce costs, length of stays, and clinician workload while improving the care teamwork environment and patient satisfaction.

IF MARKETING IS CHESS, CONTENT IS THE BACK ROW

Content is not king; it is more important than a single piece. Nothing kills a successful marketing program quicker than a weak content library.

The saying "content is king" is true, but I'd argue it's the king, queen, bishops, knights, and rooks on your marketing chessboard. Without quality content sharing your point of view or expertise, your lead-generation and brand awareness efforts will fail.

CONTENT STRATEGY

A strong content strategy is your most powerful partner in a growth journey. Strategic content marketing stands by your side every step of the way, shortening sales cycles, building brand awareness, and helping you close more business.

None of this happens if your content doesn't have purpose. That's where the right content strategy comes in.

Purposeful content marketing speaks to your prospects at every stage of the buying cycle, carving out space in their minds, and building connections.

CONTENT MAPPED TO THE BUYER JOURNEY

In setting up our clients' marketing campaigns, one of the most common questions is what content works best. The answer is it depends on what stage of the buying journey the people you are trying to reach are in.

Many B2B industries have a long sales cycle, from three months to over one year. In health care, it's not uncommon to take two or three years to close a deal. It's unlikely that a prospect who has never heard of your company will read your latest blog post and immediately decide to buy your product or service.

As a marketer, it's your job to nurture the prospects' journey and guide them. While there are many reasons that marketing campaigns underperform, one of the most frequent roadblocks to success is not having the right information in front of your buyers when they are most receptive to it.

If your buyers aren't saying "I see you everywhere," you aren't producing enough quality content.

GET TO KNOW THE 3-30-3 RULE

When it comes to your audience reading your content, you get the following:

- three seconds to grab their attention
- thirty seconds for a glance
- three minutes for a full read (if you're lucky)

Instead Of Expected Content	Try This New Format
Fact sheet	Day in the life video (of your end user)
Sales slick	Ebook
Webinar	Executive roundtable
Written case study	Customer testimonial video
User group meeting	Interactive experience

MAKING THE RIGHT MARKETING MOVES
If Marketing Is Poker, Content Is The Royal Flush

1. **Build content with a purpose.** Tie your content strategy to business goals. For example, if you are trying to differentiate your company from competitors, write a thought-leadership book (like this one).

2. **Develop content for each stage of the buyer journey.** If you only develop content for the top-of-funnel awareness stage, you won't get conversions, only hand raisers, especially in long-sales cycle markets like health care. Develop content for search, research, purchase decision, and post-sale/upsell phases.

3. **Create a starter content library before setting up marketing workflows.** I know you're itching to get out an email campaign

if you just purchased a sophisticated auto-mation system. But the content should drive marketing automation workflow, not the other way around.

4. **Grab your audience's attention with content in unexpected formats.** Lots of companies produce blogs, but not many take the time to write an ebook or host a TV show. Video and audio will become even more important now that artificial intelligence (AI) is generating content. What are ways you can stand out because you took the extra time to do something really interesting?

5. **Review your web analytics to come up with new content.** There's a gold mine in your analytics and chat data. See which topics are already resonating with your prospects and generate more content around it.

6. **Ask your sales and operations teams for ideas.** Create content that answers questions they get. We created engaging content called Ask a Scientist based on the questions that came into the purchasing department of a biologics company.

Move 13

EASY WAYS TO GENERATE MORE CONTENT WITHOUT BOTS

Remember Julie Wolk, the chief marketing officer at Carium? She is one of the most creative minds I've met in health tech marketing. In her over twenty years of marketing, including at Dell, she's learned to lean into human experience as the design driver of marketing content.

Julie advises that you need to get people from different disciplines: developers, sales, and end customers, into a room and ask them what emotion and action a feature or benefit should evoke. Marketing needs to be the dot connector more than the content originator.

Julie's team developed a "Coffee Talks with the CEO" campaign that uses images of coffee pouring and sends coffee gift cards to prospective attendees to pull in their senses. Why? "Coffee evokes conversation and comfort," says Julie, "so participants are immediately at ease and open to receive our messaging."

Carium atomized the Coffee Talks into multiple pieces of content: video, scripts, social posts, blogs, and other media to connect with health system buyer personas successfully.

FIND CONTENT THAT SPEAKS TO ALL PERSONAS

The marketing department alone cannot produce enough quality content, even with gains in AI and content-generating bots. Make creating it a performance objective for everyone in the company.

Enterprise buyers come from all departments, not just marketing. Consider a health system that wants to on-board a new patient billing system. The CIO, CTO, chief medical officer, CFO, COO, and procurement director will likely have a say in the vendor selection.

The marketing department's content may not resonate with the CFO because it misses the nuances the financial community considers impactful. The campaign using this content fails, and the leadership blames marketing.

Successful lead-generation and brand awareness campaigns demand content that speaks to each persona throughout the buyer journey. Yet, too often, the job of generating the content falls solely into the hands of marketers who don't understand the needs and challenges of the other disciplines. Everyone in the organization should be responsible for creating the content needed for lead-generation and brand awareness efforts, not just marketing.

A WORD ON CHATGPT AND AI BOTS

Beware the bots. As I'm writing this, ChatGPT is all the rage. No one truly knows at this writing how bots will change content marketing, but they will have an impact.

Bots may do marketers a favor in the long run by getting rid of bland, boring content.

The demand for content will keep growing, so everyone will need to help generate it.

As buying team numbers grow and attention spans shrink, it's critical to have personalized, accurate content at every stage of the journey for every economic buyer and influencer.

THE DEMAND FOR CONTENT WILL KEEP GROWING, SO EVERYONE WILL NEED TO HELP GENERATE IT.

Every department in your organization should believe content pieces are the power pieces in your marketing arsenal and contribute to them.

MAKING THE RIGHT MARKETING MOVES
Focus On Content, Content, Content

1. **Create a culture in which everyone has a marketing mentality.** Every department, from development through customer service, must understand it's responsible for getting the word out about their company's products and services. Not everyone has strong writing skills, but every employee has insight into different parts of the buying committee's psyche that he can share in an interview or bullet points.

Most people in the organization should have content creation goals as part of their performance objectives, especially the C-level and those interacting with customers and prospects, such as sales and technical support.

2. **Get marketers back to journalistic roots.** Content creators should have access to subject matter experts (SMEs) from multiple disciplines and interview SMEs and C-level leaders on a regular cadence.
Writers need to get back to basics by asking the five w's and an h:

- **Who** does this affect? With **whom** will this message resonate?
- **What** product feature is strongest? **What** problem does our service solve for this buyer?
- **When** will the buyer need this product? **When** did competitors first emerge?
- **Where** will our product be used inside the enterprise? **Where** are the economic and influencer buyers geographically located?
- **Why** does a particular department see our solution as crucial?
- **How** is our service solving problems now? **How** will it be critical in the future?

3. **Reach more than read/write learners with a vast array of sources.** Not everyone learns by reading, yet most of the generated content is copy-heavy blogs, briefs, and white papers.

Your target personas fall into these learning categories:

- Visual learners need to see charts and graphics to visualize information. The vast majority of the population falls into this group.
- Auditory learners need to hear information to best process it.
- Read/write learners absorb information by reading information and writing about concepts. They are the easiest to reach because marketing organizations typically have many written-word pieces in their content libraries.
- Kinesthetic learners are the toughest to reach because they learn by engaging in activities.

By tapping into a more extensive pool of knowledge within your organization, the marketing team can develop not only written content, such as blogs and white papers, but infographics, interactive graphics, videos, and podcasts.

Interview your CFO for a podcast, capture your CEO discussing brand stories on a video, run fun multidepartment activities at user group meetings and sit with engineering managers to develop interactive graphics.

4. **Atomize the heck out of every piece of content you create.** It takes a lot of effort and investment to create quality content. Break every piece of content down into smaller, more easily digestible pieces. Turn a white paper into a checklist or a top ten list into an infographic. Cut your one-minute testimonial videos into ten-second trailers.

Move 14

Andrew Lockhart was an avid basketball player, spending most of his weekends on the court with his friends. While playing a pickup game, he went up for a layup and came down awkwardly, tearing two ligaments.

He went to the nearest hospital in pain and frustration for an MRI. But when the bill came, he was shocked at the exorbitant amount he had to pay. He realized that he had gone out of network and had to pay the entire cost of the procedure, adding insult to his injury.

This experience made Andrew curious about the medical billing process. Wanting to do good in the world, he decided to use AI and machine learning to automate medical coding and help hospitals get paid accurately by insurers.

But Andrew had a big challenge as CEO of Fathom. He and his company were not well known in the health tech industry outside of a few physician investors.

Clarity Quest's public relations team got to work building Fathom's brand awareness in the revenue cycle trade publications the company's buyers read. We secured eight interviews and articles in the first months, including the cover story in the September/October 2022 issue of BC Advantage: "How To Use AI And Automation To Eliminate Coding Errors."[27]

Fathom's VP commercial operations Amit Jayakar got a lead at a trade show because someone came up to him and asked, "Oh, are you guys the ones on the cover of *BC Advantage*?"

Boom. Talk about third-party validation.

Fathom raised a series B round of $46 million in the tough funding environment of late 2022. Andrew and his team continue to refine and improve the technology, expanding its reach and positive impact on health systems' finances.

TAKE EVERY OPPORTUNITY TO AMPLIFY YOUR MESSAGE

Third-party validation is priceless and one way to get it is earned (free) media coverage in publications and blogs, and on podcasts, vlogs, and industry-specific radio shows.

Getting free coverage is part art, part science, and a lot of sweat. Like SEO rankings, it's a marathon, not a sprint. Public relations momentum takes time to build.

PAID VERSUS EARNED MEDIA

Paid media is advertising or advertorials you pay for. Think sponsored content and Google Ads and those articles in publications that have a "sponsored" label.

Earned media is coverage of a brand or product that is not paid for, such as when a company is mentioned in a news article or on a social media post by an influencer, or when your C-level spokesperson's interview appears in a trade publication or mainstream newspaper.

Both have their place, but earned media carries more weight as third-party validation.

Myth: you can easily get on the cover of mainstream publications as a start-up. The reality is the average journalist response rate to media pitches dropped by nearly 21 percent between Q3 and Q4 of 2022.[28]

WHEN YOU SHOULD INVEST IN PR

Hiring a PR agency or in-house PR experts to secure earned media placements is expensive, and you must be committed for at least a year. If your goals are solely lead generation, then PR would sit on my priority list behind digital and social media marketing. However, if you want to get acquired, raise an investment round, or increase valuation, then PR leading to earned media coverage will have a fabulous ROI.

DON'T FORGET ABOUT ANALYSTS

Getting into analyst reports from Gartner and KLAS is very powerful third-party validation. My good friend Al Salmieri was a CIO at a big health system in Seattle. Before he passed, he told me as a C-level, he only had time to worry about the top three fires on his desk. It's great advice I use daily to decide how to market to the C-suite.

But many communications departments and agencies don't pursue analyst relations because they think you must pay for coverage. You'll have a better chance of getting coverage if you are also a paid research customer, but I've had success lining up briefs for companies that were not yet customers.

As health tech marketing leader April Wilson says, "Analyst relations and PR can be the difference between making your numbers or going out of business. If your company isn't even listed on the 'best of' quadrant or annual report...you're not worth paying attention to. If you don't have attention, you don't have sales."

MAKE THE RIGHT MARKETING MOVES
Get Out Your Megaphone

1. **Create a media list.** Figure out what your buyers and influencers read and listen to. Ask current clients. Use tools like SparkToro.com to list industry influencers and journalists that visit your website, your competitor's websites, industry event sites, and publications.

2. **Ask to speak at regional trade shows and small events.** Say "yes" to small podcasts at first. Hone your craft. Record a video of your speech and guest appearance on your podcast. Then submit to speak at larger venues.

3. **Target trade publications before mainstream media.** Getting into the trades will give you validation. Unless you have a famous CEO or one with a mind-blowing story and personality, stick to trades first.

4. **Know what's trending in your industry.** At the time I'm writing this in February 2023, over 6 percent of journalists are covering the impact of ChatGPT and AI. By the time you read this, the topic will be different. Editors write about what's hot.

5. **Build relationships with editors and free-lancers.** As leading PR expert Shannon Severino says, "You need a degree in psychology to connect with some editors." Scour their social media to see what food they like, hobbies, and, most importantly, topics they cover. Make their lives easy. They have tough jobs.

6. **Don't send verbatim press releases.** Write pitches and hooks related to the press announcement instead. Then include a link to the release.

7. **SEO and earned media are a powerful combo.** Press coverage boosts SEO rankings if you are lucky enough to get a backlink to your site in the article. Always ask. On the flip side, editors may discover you through SEO rankings.

8. **Remember to brief analysts.** They need to ensure they are reviewing every valid solution and system out there.

Move 15

WHY YOUR BUSINESS NEEDS THREE TRAINED SPOKESPEOPLE

In 2021, Wayne Wager, then-CEO of Remote Medical International (RMI), scored a major publicity win, but it was "touch and go" for a bit.

RMI is a medical services company that works in remote and challenging industrial environments throughout the world. Think medics providing comprehensive medical care for workers at mining operations, on ships at sea, and on oil rigs.

The company had a sought-after service in the early days of the COVID-19 pandemic: COVID-19 testing in critical companies that had to stay open with in-person workforces, such as food processing and TV production sets.

Traditionally, RMI had not sold into these agricultural and entertainment markets, so no one knew RMI offered virus testing. The challenge was to come up with a plan to get their name out, and quickly, while companies urgently needed these services.

We hit the jackpot by using a combination of paid Google Ads (we were the first to get approval from Google to advertise for worksite testing), organic search results, and earned media outreach.

In the summer of 2021, Lauren Hirsch of the *New York Times* called for a quote from RMI with a same-day deadline.

Here's where multiple trained spokespeople came in. You don't tell the *New York Times* your client is not available.

Wager was in meetings, but we had their COO Paul Budak lined up in case the CEO couldn't break away. Ultimately, we were able to pull Wager out of his meeting to do the interview, but it was comforting to have a backup plan.

The article "Companies Desperate to Reopen Ask: What's Your Vaccination Status?" appeared on the front page of the *New York Times* business section in June 2021.[29]

What's the moral of the story? You never know when the *New York Times* will want your opinion. Have multiple trained and committed media spokespeople at the ready to communicate a consistent, impactful message and get free publicity.

BUSINESS LEADERS ARE A TRUSTED SOURCE OF INFORMATION

According to the 2023 Edelman Trust Barometer, in a world that is divided into opposing sides, businesses stand out as the only trustworthy entities when compared to NGOs, governments, and the media. Moreover, CEOs are identified as one of the most reliable sources of information. These results emphasize the significance of effective communication skills for contemporary leaders, as they have the chance to establish trust and establish rapport with crucial stakeholders.[30]

BE PREPARED TO SPEAK

In 1897, Winston Churchill famously wrote:

> Of all the talents bestowed upon men, none is so precious as the gift of oratory. He who enjoys it wields a power more durable than that of a great king. He is an independent force in the world. Abandoned by his party, betrayed by his friends, stripped of his offices, whoever can command this power is still formidable.[31]

Dynamic speakers in your organization are a competitive advantage. Consider two biotech companies selling similar services.

The CEO of Company A is on stage at premier industry trade shows, speaks quarterly to analysts, is a regular contributor to trade publications, and responds to all quality media requests for interviews, even at the drop of a hat. She regularly appears on podcasts and onstage panels.

The CEO of Company B focuses on financials, operations, and acquisition growth strategies. Publicity is not top-of-mind, and he doesn't make the time to respond to last-minute interviews unless it's the *New York Times* or *Wall Street Journal*.

His salespeople don't meet their targets because Company B's prospects have never heard of them, and the sales teams have to justify why they are different and better than Company A.

Guess which company has an easier time getting the attention of senior buyers? Which has a higher valuation? You got it. Company A.

WHY YOUR COMPANY NEEDS TRAINED AND RELIABLE MEDIA SPOKESPEOPLE

I frequently hear from frustrated sales leaders that a competitor's CEO is outshining theirs and making it harder for them to close.

There are so many media opportunities given every publication, blog, podcast, and conference needs quality content. You don't want your C-level getting bogged down on the lower-level channels. Plus, reporters often need a quote or interview on very short notice.

So have trained spokespeople available at different levels of your organization and assign appearances based on the seniority level needed. Everyone will want to speak to the CEO, but that's not feasible.

WHAT IS MEDIA SPOKESPERSON TRAINING?

Media spokesperson training helps individuals responsible for representing a company or organization to the media effectively communicate with reporters and the public. Training can be provided through various means, including in-person training sessions, online courses, or one-on-one coaching.

Media spokesperson training will help your spokespeople prepare for interviews, effectively convey the company's message, respond to difficult questions, and handle media interviews professionally.

Some specific skills that may be covered in media spokesperson training include:

- **Message development.** Developing clear and concise messaging that accurately reflects the company's position on various issues.
- **Interview techniques.** Learning how to effectively handle media interviews, answering difficult questions, and staying on message.
- **Presentation skills.** Developing the ability to present information clearly and confidently in front of a camera or microphone.
- **Crisis communication.** Learning how to respond to negative situations or crises in a way that minimizes damage to the company's reputation.
- **Media relationships.** Building and maintaining positive relationships with reporters and other members of the media.

ENGAGE IN DIFFERENT FORMATS

If one of your founders has an effective origin or disruption story, get him to convey it consistently and often in different mediums—written, verbal, and auditory. Different people learn and retain information in various ways.

DO YOU NEED A CELEBRITY SPOKESPERSON OR PATIENT ADVOCATE?

Short answer: yes. We live in an influencer society, even in the B2B ecosystem.

MAKING THE RIGHT
MARKETING MOVES

Control Your Narrative With The Power Of Three

Having assigned and trained media spokespeople is necessary for several additional reasons:

1. **Master your messaging.** An assigned spokesperson can help ensure that your company's messages are consistent and accurately convey the company's positioning.

2. **Share your expertise.** Spokespeople who are trained and knowledgeable about the company and its operations can provide more accurate, timely, and comprehensive information to the media.

3. **Build credibility.** Designated spokespeople who are familiar with the company and its operations are more credible than paid spokespeople or public relations agency representatives who rely on talking points.

4. **Respond quickly.** Having several assigned spokespeople allows your company to respond quickly and effectively to media inquiries, which can help control the narrative around the company and minimize the potential for negative publicity.

5. **Establish trust.** Trained spokespeople can help maintain a professional image for your company. Media will come to recognize your

organization as a reliable source, and as your PR footprint grows, your target audience will come to recognize the thought leadership you provide.

6. **Practice makes perfect.** Build media interview skills by running through practice scenarios with trained PR coaches.

Move 16

TOP OF THE TOWER: FILLING YOUR PIPELINE WITH LEAD GENERATION

This is a cautionary tale.

Dave Smith (true story, but name changed for confidentiality reasons) was the CEO of a healthcare software company selling billing services into physician practices. When we calculated the funnel needed, it turned out the total available specialty practices market was not big enough to meet the company's revenue goals.

The company's marketing program and its associated budget was going to have to expand to include primary care and internal medicine practices. And Dave just didn't have the money to do this at the level needed to be successful. He needed to get additional funding, but he refused to because it would dilute his shares.

So, the company plodded along, stalled because they are sales-driven, not marketing-empowered.

DID YOU SKIP TO THIS CHAPTER?

If you've skipped to this chapter, stop. Right now.
Founders and CEOs often want to leapfrog all the hard work that builds the marketing foundation. But lead generation is at the top of the Tower Of Power for a reason: you

can't generate quality leads at the volume needed on the back of shoddy branding, strategy, and content.

Once you've built a solid marketing foundation, then you're ready to fill your pipeline.

DETERMINING HOW MANY LEADS YOU NEED

Many CEOs are shocked at the large number of leads that marketing needs to generate at the top-of-the-funnel (hand raisers) to result in the desired number of conversions to the bottom of the funnel. Some realize too late that their total available market is too small, or they'd have to capture 90 percent of the market to meet their revenue goals.

Here's a traditional sales funnel we created as part of market research for a biopharmaceutical services company that needed just eight new customer logos coming from marketing each year (each were six-figure engagements). The sales team had separate goals.[32]

If you work up from conversions to the engaged prospects needed at the top of the funnel, they needed to engage 555 pharmaceutical companies. There are 2,655 brand name pharmaceutical manufacturing businesses in the US as of 2023 so this company needed a marketing budget that would reach 21 percent of the total available market. You can't do that on the cheap.

A Traditional Funnel Used Solely For The
Purpose of Target Market Calculations

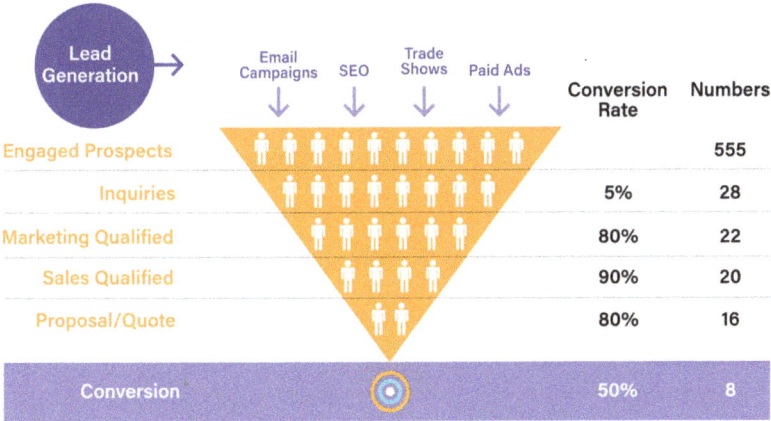

	Email Campaigns	SEO	Trade Shows	Paid Ads	Conversion Rate	Numbers
Lead Generation →						
Engaged Prospects						555
Inquiries					5%	28
Marketing Qualified					80%	22
Sales Qualified					90%	20
Proposal/Quote					80%	16
Conversion					50%	8

CHOOSING YOUR LEAD-GENERATION CHANNELS

Once you know how many first-touch leads you need from marketing, it's time to select which marketing channels to invest in. This is where a skilled marketing leader or agency can really help make sure you don't waste time and money.

Successful channels for your business depend on many factors such as whether you are selling products or services and how many people are involved in buying decisions at your prospective companies.

Plus, don't forget about nurturing those top-of-funnel leads if you are in a long sales cycle industry like selling software into health systems.

MAKING THE RIGHT
MARKETING MOVES
All The Right Lead-Gen Channels

I like these channels for all B2B healthcare, life sciences, and tech companies:

1. **LinkedIn sponsored content ads.** These ads appear in the feeds of LinkedIn users that you can very specifically target by company size, location, title, etc. For educational sales (most tech B2B sales), LinkedIn can't be beat for getting top-of-funnel leads and brand awareness.

2. **Search engine rankings.** Structure your website to rank highly on search engine results and consistently put quality content on it so you show up on page one for competitive search terms.

3. **Email workflows.** Use automated email workflows to nurture prospects that have already engaged with you. Get them to take the next step after downloading an asset such as signing up for a webinar, researcher roundtable, or concierge suite event you're hosting. Caution: don't go buy a list and spam people. It's now against the law in many countries and states, and it annoys people.

4. **Social media.** Get a social media marketing tool and link your company's leadership

profiles to it. Send out consistent content from leadership, not just over your corporate profiles. Your leaders typically have many more followers than the corporate brand unless you are at the enterprise level.

5. **Lead-generation programs run by validated third-party publications.** These are expensive but if your audience reads a technical journal or trade magazine and trusts it, the lead quality coming out of these can have good ROI. Make sure you don't have to pay for students and consultants as part of the lead-generation fee. Negotiate this up front.

Move 17

RIGHT SIZE AND RIGHT SKILLS: HIRING YOUR MARKETING DEPARTMENT

As the former chief clinical operations officer at Teladoc, Alan Roga, MD, knew how important marketing foundation was to a successful company launch.

His company, TruLite Health, is tackling the audacious goal of eliminating inequities in health care. They created an industry-first, enterprise-wide health equity platform built to address racial and ethnic health disparities at the point of care.

Alan needed first-mover advantage in the minds of potential buyers as large electronic health record companies were also developing health equity technology. But that required a branding team ready to make the moves.

He knew it would have taken him six months to hire and onboard a marketing team and at least another quarter to finish the foundational work.

By partnering with an agency, Alan was able to quickly launch and gain leadership positioning with health systems, including at historically Black colleges and universities (HBCUs).

Clarity Quest developed brand messaging, brand architecture, product naming, sales collateral, an investor deck, and a new website in less than four months, meeting their desired company launch timeline.

YOUR MARKETING IS ONLY AS GOOD AS YOUR TEAM

Whether you are a start-up with a team of one, or a meg-acap enterprise, a successful marketing department requires an ever-increasing range of creative and analytical talents. Here's a breakdown of the roles needed and when you'll need them based on the size of your company.

MARKETING LEADER (CMO, VP MARKETING)

You need a marketing leadership function unless you fully outsource your marketing department to an agency that provides an acting CMO. If you are a start-up, hire a marketing vice president to run the show. You simply won't have enough time as a CEO to oversee marketing.

Many companies hire a VP of sales and marketing, which is a mistake. Ninety-nine percent of the time a VP of sales and marketing is from sales and does not understand or value the marketing function in an organization.

In over twenty years of working with companies, I've only met one unicorn chief commercial officer who effectively led the marketing and sales functions simultaneously. Hire a true marketing leader that can interface with the sales team and not be beholden to it.

The marketing leader should handle the multiyear marketing plan and submit an annual budget. She should lead the marketing audit annually and have authority to hire and fire marketing staff and agencies.

CONTENT CREATORS

You'll never have enough content, so either hire content talent in-house or get an agency familiar with your vertical on a recurring monthly contract. Many companies understaff the content team or don't budget enough to outsource the amount of content needed.

You'll need content for your website, digital ad campaigns, SEO, social media campaigns, email workflows, and internal and external communications. If you pursue public relations, many publications are understaffed and will ask you to provide copy for earned media placements.

GRAPHIC DESIGN

Graphic designers will add the visual punch to the copy your content team writes.

Hire an agency on a graphic design retainer or hire this function in-house. It's a mistake to think you can find an agency that can deliver work successfully on an ad hoc basis. Agencies are not staffed with graphic designers sitting around waiting for project work to come in. They are on recurring revenue contracts unless they are between assignments.

WEB DESIGN AND DEVELOPMENT

While hosting and the domain name system can be managed by your IT department, it's essential that marketing control the content, design, and user interface of the corporate website and microsites. Get someone on your team who can interface between IT and the creative side of the marketing house.

DIGITAL MARKETING

Digital encompasses a huge part of your marketing department, as a vital driver of lead generation. Make sure you have experts in:

- SEO
- Organic and paid social marketing
- Search engine marketing (SEM), paid search
- Marketing automation and email marketing
- Account-based marketing (if implemented for B2B)
- Programmatic advertising

TRADE SHOW MANAGEMENT

In-person events are back and shouldn't be ignored. Even a small booth requires planning and logistics that are best managed by a person dedicated to the task if you attend more than a few shows a year.

ANALYTICS

While many companies lump analytics into digital marketing, it's so important now that it deserves a separate department and leader once you are out of series B.[33] Marketing has to prove return-on-investment, show attribution to the bottom line, and know where to spend next, so it's critical to make decisions based on readily available data.

PUBLIC RELATIONS

Public relations covers earned media, reputation management, and crisis management. And while your PR team may recommend paid media, the budget for paid media placements usually falls into digital marketing or traditional advertising.

A seasoned PR leader can help set the marketing strategy, interface with the content team, submit solid speaker abstracts, and communicate to the media. She should have connections in at least regional and trades for B2B organizations, and national media for larger B2B and B2C.

Earned and paid media helps raise the brand awareness of your company. I love this channel if you are pursuing an exit within three years and want to raise your valuation. But it's not a short-term lead-generation channel, and many CEOs incorrectly view it as such.

INTERNAL COMMUNICATIONS

Once your company passes the 500-person mark, you'll most likely want an internal communications director/manager to ensure everyone remains on the same page on brand messaging and mission.

A QUICK NOTE ON HIRING FOR VALUES VS. SKILLS

While the first part of this chapter concentrated on the skills needed for each marketing discipline, I'd be remiss if I didn't mention you won't always find the skills you need to hire, but you can always find recruits willing to learn who share your values.

Leadership often makes the mistake of considering candidates with "x years" of experience in their industry. In rapidly growing fields, such as AI and healthcare, there just aren't enough experienced candidates.

At Clarity Quest, we hired a content marketer with no healthcare experience, but she had several years of experience working at financial technology companies. We thought knowledge of fintech was close enough to health tech for her to come up to speed quickly.

We gave her a healthcare writing assignment as part of her interview process, and she nailed it. Within two years, she was recognized as a Marketing Rising Star by the Healthcare and IT Marketing Community (HITMC).

Figure out your corporate values and then make sure you hire people that can easily demonstrate how they live them out. If they are highly experienced in your industry, look at that experience as a bonus.

MAKING THE RIGHT MARKETING MOVES
Rightsize Your Marketing Team

1. **Decide on an in-house or outsourced marketing model.** While building an internal marketing empire may seem attractive, it's not always the most cost-efficient play.
2. **If hiring in-house, start with a marketing leadership position.** Too many companies

make the mistake of hiring a graphic designer or content manager and having them report to the CEO or VP sales. This recipe sinks marketing programs unless there's super tight sales and marketing alignment and an equal respect for both disciplines (which I've found in all of two sales leaders over twenty-two years).

3. **Understand one person can't do all things marketing.** The skills required for marketing excellence are extremely diverse. Don't expect a talented graphic designer to get earned media coverage. Expecting one person to be a jack-of-all-trades will lead the person to burn out quickly because there's no way he can succeed at everything required.

4. **Hire for values first.** In a competitive talent marketplace, you may not be able to find candidates from your industry. Hire for the right mindset and comparable values, and provide all the training new employees need.

5. **Don't park the responsibility for your website in IT.** Yes, your IT department should make sure the website is safe and secure from hackers and corruption. But the day-to-day site updates should rest with a webmaster that lives in marketing. IT is too mired in firefighting security and compliance issues.

Move 18

Faye Espiritu was the senior director of marketing at a healthcare technology company providing a critical role in solving the nursing shortage hospitals face. Faye is supersmart with a strong work ethic, but she didn't know the ins and outs of marketing into health systems, having come from general tech.

Faye knew when to ask for help and convinced her CEO to hire an agency team to mentor her through the areas of healthcare marketing she didn't know well.

"Having industry veterans as mentors and consultants helped me put together a plan to scale my organization and bring it to the next level as we raised funding rounds," said Faye. "We took apart everything, including the organization charts, and found ways to improve it."

In addition to auditing her marketing plan and budget, we weighed in on her planned organization chart and hiring plans. This gave the company a solid marketing Tower of Power that survived even after Faye decided to leave her position.

THE POWER OF A
GREAT AGENCY PARTNERSHIP

"I've been burned in the past by a bad agency" is a common refrain I hear from CEOs. An unsuccessful partnership can throw money down the drain at a fast clip, leaving both the client and agency frustrated.

But a great agency partnership can bring unparalleled creativity and results in record time.

So how do you get into the great agency partnership camp? Know what you want to accomplish and how you work.

KNOW AND SHARE CLEAR GOALS

If you start the first call with an agency with, "We're not sure what we want," and then proceed to nix every idea, all kinds of alarm bells go off at the agency. Be prepared to communicate what success looks like for a partnership.

Before talking to prospective agencies, figure out if you want a strategic, tactical, or hybrid partner. Agencies should be able to clearly articulate which lane they occupy.

Marketing is not accounting. Marketing is messy, fun, and creative. It's finger paint mixed with logic. Gray matter and data analysis exist simultaneously. If you don't have anything in common with the

> MARKETING IS NOT ACCOUNTING. MARKETING IS MESSY, FUN, AND CREATIVE. IT'S FINGER PAINT MIXED WITH LOGIC.

agency's team members, it's going to be tough to clear hurdles and work through challenges.

KNOW YOUR WORK STYLE

If you need to speak to a marketing expert every day or want to constantly bounce marketing ideas off someone, an agency is going to frustrate you. News flash: you are not the agency's only client. You're better off hiring in-house.

THE CASE AGAINST GENERALIST AGENCIES

While they may come at a discount, generalist agencies have the highest failure rate. Choosing a generalist agency because they are located in your city may seem sane. They are right around the corner if you need to meet.

But in today's remote work world, location matters less and less.

What's important is hiring an agency that intimately knows your industry, its quirks, and what works to get you results. Generalist agencies are going to have to A/B test[34] like crazy, wasting your time and treasure.

MAKING THE RIGHT MARKETING MOVES
Making Friends With The Right Agency

Use these tips for selecting an agency that fits your organization like a glove, lowering the risk of hiring the wrong agency.

1. **Have a clear vision of what you want the agency to accomplish.** Know what success will look like in six months and one year if you engage. For example, do you need strategic direction or more tactical hands on deck? Are you trying to increase brand awareness or demand generation?

2. **Don't use a surrogate to vet your agencies.** If you rely on your equity partner or a consultant to find an agency, there's no guarantee you will like working with them, or the agency will like working with you. Venture capitalists, investors, and consultants have different agendas and different work styles than your company. They might not know the right questions to ask. Make the time to meet and interview agencies yourself.

3. **Qualify the agency on your terms.** You don't have to issue twenty-page requests for proposals (RFPs) to find the right agency. You might be more comfortable with in-person meetings, web meetings, or phone conversations. We have successful, long-term relationships with clients that selected us after two phone calls and some that involved a multimonth sales process. However, the ones that involved coffee, lunch, and a pitch meeting are often the longest lasting.

4. **Don't release a huge RFP with a tight deadline.** Many boutique, vertically-focused agencies don't participate in RFPs or will participate only if there are limited competitors, a reasonable timeline, or a perceived perfect fit. If you blast a huge RFP with a supertight response deadline, you will get responses from agencies that are not busy. Those are probably not the agencies you want.

5. **Ask references if they hold the same values.** If you're obsessed with timely delivery or otherworldly creativity, then be sure to ask references for specific examples of how the agency provided those things. Don't only ask if the agency filled their sales funnel.

6. **Connect on levels outside of business.** Over the long haul, issues arise no matter how great both parties are. It will be much easier to overcome hurdles if you have some hobbies or real-life experiences in common. Some of our best client partnerships survived tough times because we had a mutual passion for yoga, tasty sangria, a nonprofit, or kayaking. A trusted relationship, not just an engagement, leads to a true partnership that weathers storms.

7. **Communicate with transparency to your internal staff.** The executive should make it clear to any existing staff that the agency is

not replacing them, but is simply seeking an extension of the team. It would be similar if you were to outsource other strategic functional areas, such as accounting. Involve your internal staff in the selection process.

8. **Set a realistic budget.** If you set a budget too low, you set yourself and the agency up for failure. A good agency will inform you during the sales process if your expectations are not in line with your approved spending.

9. **Trust the agency you choose.** You don't need to be involved in every small decision regarding copywriting and graphic design. Give meaningful, detailed feedback to your agency team and then let them fly.

10. **Trust your gut and don't settle.** If you get to the final selection round and are not crazy about any of the agencies, don't hire one out of a sense of obligation to the process. You'll have immediate buyer's remorse. It's better for both parties that you spend the time looking for another agency or consider hiring in-house.

Once you find the right marketing agency, you'll be astounded at how much you can accomplish. You'll have more brainpower, more strategic thinking, a savvy outsider's viewpoint, and more hands on deck. You'll be glad you took the time at the beginning to vet the right partner.

Move 19

OUTSOURCING YOUR MARKETING CAN BE OUTSTANDING

RMI had tried staffing its marketing function in-house for years.

Its then-COO, Paul Budak, was frustrated because they consistently lost marketing team members to bigger companies in the area, namely Amazon and Microsoft.

He finally convinced the board and leadership it would be easier for an agency to provide turnkey marketing versus hiring in-house staff. They contracted with Clarity Quest for almost three years until the company moved overseas.

The benefit? They saw a better performance by outsourcing with our agency.

Budak said, "Compared to our previous internal marketing team, the Clarity Quest outsource team really filled the funnel with a higher ROI than anyone expected."

Former CEO Wayne Wager added, "You allowed RMI to reduce marketing expenses while you significantly increased marketing productivity. The leads being generated from the website are impressive."

But is this the right marketing move for everyone?

OUTSOURCED MARKETING GAINED TRACTION

Twenty-five years ago, CEOs typically didn't think of outsourcing their marketing department. On the West Coast, where I started Clarity Quest, outsourced marketing was gaining traction, but it was still a bold concept.

Today, we get inquiries from multiple companies each month that want to completely outsource their marketing function.

Why the change?

MARKETING REQUIRES SPECIALIZED EXPERTISE

If you've ever been stumped by LinkedIn Campaign Manager or perplexed why Google rejected your ad copy, you've experienced the need for specialization firsthand. Effective marketing requires expertise in strategy, tech, content, design, and analytics. Throw in public relations, and that's another required universe of particular skill sets.

IT'S TOUGH TO FIND QUALITY CANDIDATES, AND THEY ARE EXPENSIVE

B2B marketing pros with experience in your industry demand a higher price than generalists and are tough to hire postpandemic. Please know that 30 percent won't even show up for their interview.

Average Marketing Compensation as of January 2023						
Job Title	Average Annual Salary		Average Benefits Costs		Total Compensation	
	PayScale	Glassdoor	PayScale	Glassdoor	PayScale	Glassdoor
Chief Marketing Officer[35, 36]	$178,447	$177,901	$131,500	$168,137	$309,947	$346,038
Content Marketing Manager[37,38]	$72,333	$67,265	$18,244	$6,523	$90,577	$73,788
Marketing Technology Manager[39,40]	$92,974	$94,988	$8,500	$23,024	$101,474	$118,012
Marketing Director[41,42]	$94,178	$109,907	$45,000	$50,990	$139,178	$160,897
Marketing Strategist[43,44]	$64,483	$57,817	$46,627	$19,245	$111,110	$77,062
Marketing Analyst[45,46]	$59,639	$62,473	$32,748	$4,728	$92,387	$67,201
Graphic Designer[47,48]	$49,092	$44,257	$11,483	$2,332	$60,575	$46,589
Digital Marketing Manager[49, 50]	$71,540	$71,026	$32,725	$7,003	$104,265	$78,029
Total for Team of Specialists	$682,686	$685,634	$326,827	$281,982	$1,009,513	$967,616

Can you afford to staff all of that marketing expertise internally? Most small and medium businesses cannot. Once staff members are onboarded, they are constantly being approached by recruiters.

EMPLOYEE CHURN

Unless you have an all-star culture and you work every day to maintain it, you will experience churn. It's not uncommon for in-house marketers to leave after only six months—just when they start to give you a return on the investment you made in them.

OBJECTIVE RECOMMENDATIONS

It's easy to miss opportunities because "it's the way we've always done it." The fresh perspective of an outsourced team can be invaluable when brainstorming solutions to tough hurdles.

SCALABLE BUDGETS

By outsourcing, your company pays only for the services used for the length of time needed. The marketing team assigned to your firm can be scaled to suit projects of any size and scope. With an in-house team, you have consistent overhead and expenses.

ACCESS TO THE LATEST TOOLS AND TECHNOLOGY

Marketing agencies often have access to the latest marketing tech stacks, enabling them to deliver more effective marketing strategies. Plus, you'll be able to cost share the tools with their other clients.

MARKETING NEEDS CHANGE OVER TIME

As your company grows and market conditions change, strategy and campaign execution requirements evolve. Even over the course of just a year, it's difficult to predict exactly what skills you'll need.

A full-service agency with a wide range of expertise under one roof can flex with your company as you grow or even merge with another company.

TIME TO FOCUS ON YOUR CORE COMPETENCIES

By outsourcing the marketing function, your internal team will have more time to spend on what you do best. For example, tech companies will have more time for research, development, and customer support.

WHY STRATEGIC OUTSOURCED MARKETING MAKES SENSE FOR TECHNOLOGY FIRMS

With its attractive advantages, marketing outsourcing might be assumed to be a logical choice for nearly every company looking to grow its business. But certain key characteristics of technology firms make strategic outsourced marketing extremely attractive.

Technology firms must focus on their intellectual property and product life cycles, and often cannot focus on the latest in marketing tactics.

Today's volatile business environment requires access to resources well-versed in current practices across all marketing disciplines. Outsourcing the marketing function lets key executives in the firm focus on the core competencies instead of trying to keep up on the latest marketing strategies and devoting resources to recruitment and retention.

MAKING THE RIGHT MARKETING MOVES
Opt For Outside-The-Box Outsourcing

1. **Consider outsourcing your entire marketing team.** Previously seen as bizarre, outsourcing and virtual CMOs have proven to be an effective way to field a marketing team. Especially if you want to exit in less than three years.

2. **Deal with hiring and turnover by outsourcing.** When you're a small-to-midsized company, like RMI, holding on to marketing talent will be tough. Agencies with vertical expertise can devise a strategy and execute the campaigns within weeks, not months or years.

3. **Get access to a quality marketing tech stack.** Marketing automation, reputation management, social sharing, and new AI tools are expensive. Agencies can share the costs among multiple clients getting you great tech at a fraction of the cost.

4. **Get objective viewpoints.** You're often too close to your baby to see what really needs to be done. An agency can call out a bad message or campaign idea. At least

give them an audience, even if you decide against their advice.

5. **Stay away from agencies if you're a micro-manager.** Or if you need daily updates and brainstorm sessions. Unless you've partnered with an agency on a high-end, exclusive contract, you will be sharing resources with other clients. You should expect deliverables by promised dates and scheduled meetings, but agencies can't often drop everything to discuss things daily.

6. **Don't outsource without clear goals and a marketing plan.** If the agency doesn't understand what you view as success, they'll never get there. If you don't have mapped goals, strategic agencies can help you develop them.

Move 20

MARKET LIKE ATHLETES, NOT WEEKEND WARRIORS

I gave up running for the longest time because I kept getting shin splints and sharp knee pain.

The problem? I'd been running only twice a week. But when I started daily interval training, I could run twenty to thirty minutes daily without pain.

During one guided workout, my digital trainer coached, "Don't worry that you're only running for twenty minutes. Consistency trumps intensity every time."

The same goes for marketing. Consistency trumps intensity every time.

MARKETING WEEKEND WARRIORS

Marketing teams can fall into the same cycle of intense effort followed by exhaustion and exasperation. Consider these common marketing weekend warrior scenarios:

- **Launch warriors** focus their time and effort on a new offering, then quickly lose steam a few weeks after the launch—when leads need nurturing.
- **Big-event warriors** spend months planning for a big conference and then fail to follow up, engage, and nurture attendees after the event.

- **New-tool warriors** get excited about the latest technology stack or app but fail to create enough original content to feed the tools successfully.
- **Content-blitz warriors** develop an initial content set but fail to develop new pieces or update content with new information or customer input.
- **Goal warriors** aim for transformation far exceeding what an organization can realistically implement in a short period—and fall short.

In *Predictions 2019: Transformation Goes Pragmatic*, Forrester details that many organizations had unsuccessful 2018 customer experience (CX) and digital channel campaigns because they set unrealistic goals for the size or maturity of their organization.[51] And as a consequence of that initial failure, Forrester predicted 25 percent of firms will decelerate digital efforts and will lose market share; also, 20 percent will eliminate CX initiatives in favor of price cuts to attract customers and maintain volumes—which, as we all know, is not a long-term growth strategy.

MAKING THE RIGHT MARKETING MOVES
Adopt A Marketing Training Regimen To Avoid Burnout

1. **Create and implement a marketing training plan.** Long-distance runners review a map before the race. You should follow a planned outline with an associated budget even if you're a start-up adopting a lean or guerilla

marketing strategy. You'll have a much more detailed plan if you are an enterprise with mature marketing processes.

Everyone on the marketing team should understand the high-level business goals of the organization, and marketing's strategies and objectives should align with those of the business.

2. **Set a realistic pace.** If you set unrealistic cadence expectations for your team's size and budget, marketing burnout will likely result. For example, instead of trying to launch in multiple verticals at once and spreading a limited budget too thin, become a known brand in one market; then attack on other fronts, with cash flow supporting penetration into other verticals.

3. **Ask for help.** Top athletes know when to seek physical therapy. Some marketers, though, are afraid to ask their leaders for support, even when management announces an unplanned big event or deadline.

    Let your leadership team know if you need outsourcing or temporary assistance for a big product launch, additional show, or *schedule.* One study compared the calories burned during thirty minutes each of high-intensity interval training (HIIT), weight training, running, and biking.

The researchers found that HIIT burned 25–30 percent more calories than the other forms of exercise.[52] Again, consistency trumps intensity to get the most out of muscles and brains.

5. **Develop both timely and enduring content.** Your customers want diverse types of content to digest. Developing content that has longevity, such as an ebook with use cases, will help fill the gaps when you have event blitzes that consume much of your resources.

    However, don't rely only on durable content. Today's fast-paced business environment also requires your company to stay relevant with real-time pieces, such as blog posts and product updates.

6. **Prepare for big events at least nine months out.** You wouldn't start training for a marathon two weeks before the race. Even though exhibit booth space is often the most expensive line item in your marketing budget, many companies start to plan for a significant trade-show presence only three months before the event.

    You cannot successfully choose a theme, select messaging channels, line up public relations and analyst interviews, and launch successful booth draw campaigns in such a short time frame. Companies that exceed show goals plan the next event before the current one ends, especially at shows where prime booth locations are in demand.

For a monthly show planning cadence guide, check out *The Countdown To HIMSS Is On! Are You Getting Ready?,* which details planning steps for a large health technology show; however, the majority of the content applies to any large conference with exhibitors.[53]

Skip the last-minute blitzes before launches or events. They lead to sloppy work, resource burnout, and ineffective campaigns. Take the time to plan and work on a reasonable schedule to keep your marketing team at the top of their game for creativity and effectiveness.

Move 21

PATIENCE IS A MANDATORY MARKETING VIRTUE

Bob (true story, name changed) founded a healthcare data analytics company. His team spent five years developing an innovative SaaS product to market into pharmaceutical companies. Venture capitalists were happy to give them money for research and development.

But no one ever brought up marketing other than a rudimentary website that was built to get more investment.

A year before launch, leadership hired a sales team with nothing to sell, so the salespeople left.

Six months before launch, the company hired a new sales team and marketing operations person who quickly became overloaded. Before the official launch party, the only "marketing" they had was a small website, sales slicks, and a press release announcing the company's funding.

They launched a tactical buffet of unrelated top-of-funnel marketing campaigns (random acts of marketing) totally untied to business goals. The lead quality was poor, and there was no nurturing, so sales blamed marketing, and the marketing team got fired.

This scenario happens over and over again. And it's the quickest way to failure.

PITIFUL PLANNING PRODUCES POOR PERFORMANCE

I'm astounded when the same companies that have spent years developing a new software platform expect to launch a marketing program in six months or less. But it happens all the time.

Prospects routinely contact my agency six months before they want to launch a company or new product. And then, they expect marketing to generate qualified leads in bunches in the first month after campaign launch. It rarely works.

You can launch crappy marketing campaigns in weeks. But top-performing lead-generation and media coverage programs take time to plan. Time to A/B test. Time to get enough content to run email workflows. Time for prospects to see you for the seventh, eighteenth, or thirteenth time.

MAKING THE RIGHT MARKETING MOVES
Good Things Come To Those Who Plan

1. **Start developing a lead-generation plan twelve months before beta launch.** Don't wait until three months before intended launch. One caveat: if you're splash launching at a huge trade show, like HIMSS, VIVE, or BIO, then start at least eighteen months ahead of the show.

2. **Give digital ad campaigns at least three months to perform.** You'll probably need to A/B test, change bidding strategies, and change content if your first campaigns bomb. Great marketing has an element of trial and error.

3. **Allow six months for SEO ranking improvements.** Getting top organic rankings on Google page one, especially for competitive terms, takes time. However, if you are patient, it will pay huge dividends because it's hard and impatient companies give up.

4. **Give earned media public relations at least six months.** Editorial calendars get set on twelve-month cadences. And hot topics change daily. Even a stellar PR team will need ramp-up time to build buzz momentum, first in trade publications and then in mainstream media.

Move 22

AUDIT IS NOT A DIRTY WORD

Remember Faye Espiritu, senior director of marketing at the healthcare technology company?

In addition to auditing her organization chart, she needed healthcare marketing experts to validate her goals, objectives, and budget.

Clarity Quest provided recommendations on which campaigns to keep and which to cut, based on our experience. This gave Faye the confidence to lobby the CEO and the VP of finance for the investment required.

She got the budget and resources she needed to succeed because she followed an analytical process, which is what an audit is all about.

A IS FOR AUDIT AND ANALYSIS

The word audit may strike fear in the hearts of taxpayers, but it shouldn't scare marketers. Conducting an audit of your marketing department can be a fruitful exercise that shows leadership and investors that you know how to sharpen the pencil and get analytical.

THE MAIN REASON TO AUDIT YOUR MARKETING DEPARTMENT

Finance departments undergo annual reviews, but too few marketing departments bother to do the same. If you want marketing to be an integral part of your business, you must hold it accountable.

Your company's success rests on the quality of your marketing strategy and its execution. You can benefit from a structured audit process if you have a marketing budget of $50,000 or $50 million. I've audited marketing departments that range from B2B start-ups to Fortune 50 companies.

AN AUDIT FRAMEWORK

Here's an actionable framework that can turn a marketing audit from a "root canal experience" to an exercise your team will value. Each topic contains a list of questions you can use to guide your audit.

Setting Objectives

Set metrics and routinely measure against them. Use Goal POST—performance, objectives, strategies, and tactics— to ensure marketing understands high-level business objectives and your executive team knows marketing's KPIs.

Key Questions

- Are you clear on high-level business objectives from the C-level and expectations from marketing?
- Have you set Goal POST metrics?

- How do your key metrics compare with best-in-class companies and competitors?

Budget And ROI Assessment

Many marketing departments submit a budget to management that is merely an increase above the previous year's budget—with padding to compensate for standard cost cutting. However, you should assess whether you are spending money on the highest ROI campaigns and most fruitful events.

Attribution systems, such as Adobe Marketo Measure and Demandbase, make assigning ROI at the campaign and tactical levels easier than ever.

Key Questions

- What factors are you using to calculate your marketing budget?
- Are you attributing revenue to marketing programs? If so, does your model need to be evaluated?
- Can you eliminate programs without affecting KPIs?

Resources Evaluation

As companies grow, they too often try to pile more and more responsibilities onto the same set of people. It's vital to assess your team each year for satisfaction, availability, and skill levels.

- Is your marketing team passionate about your company and your objectives?

- Do you have the right people in roles in which they can deliver but are still able to learn and grow?
- Do you need to hire or downsize your marketing department?
- Do you need to involve an outsourced marketing agency more or less?

Demand Generation (Inbound/Outbound)

As sexier outbound channels emerge, it's easy to relegate your inbound efforts, such as search engine optimization (SEO) and funnel nurturing, to the marketing dungeon. But you should set them free instead: they are (probably) still your top source of qualified leads.

- Does your organization have the optimal ratio of inbound and outbound programs?
- On which area of the sales funnel/process are campaigns focused? For example, are you concentrating too much on volume leads at the top of the funnel when your real issue is the conversion of sales-qualified leads?
- How do your metrics compare with industry averages and best-in-class marketing companies? For example, are at least 35 percent of conversions coming from marketing?

Content Marketing Audit

With inbound playing such an essential role in successful marketing efforts, you must evaluate your content library.

- Which content types or individual pieces have garnered the most engagement?
- Do you have enough content to support current and future marketing programs and cadences?
- Is the quality of your content gold or crap? Do an honest in-house evaluation and ask your customers.

Lead Management, Sales Integration, And Sales Enablement Processes

When evaluating your marketing department, remember sales and marketing functional alignment. With processes such as account-based marketing (ABM) taking off in B2B marketing, the two departments must have open and metrics-driven communication channels.

- Are your current funnel definitions and metrics in need of an update?
- What can sales and marketing do as a team to improve lead conversion?
- Are leads falling through the cracks at any point in the sales cycle?
- Does the sales team need improved sales enablement materials or processes from marketing? What about competitive and customer research?
- What can be done to shorten sales cycles?

Social And PR Evaluations

Social and PR go hand-in-hand because they both get the word out and invite interaction.

- What's the optimal channel mix between social and PR efforts? Given your sales and business objectives, which channel should you prioritize?
- Are you using each social channel to its maximum potential? If not, should you focus on one channel where most of your customers are versus "spreading the peanut butter too thin" across three to five channels?
- Has your PR media contact list been updated in the last six months? How about your editorial calendar?

Technology Stack And Database Health

Gone are the days when marketing departments didn't need to worry about data, analytics, and tool sets. However, too often marketing groups purchase a tool and use only a small portion of its capabilities, or workflows become overly complicated.

- What's the optimal software configuration for your organization?
- Are there tools you own or subscribe to that you don't use? What can you eliminate to simplify workflows?
- When was the last time you cleaned sales and marketing databases? Have you paused campaigns to contacts that haven't engaged in a particular time frame?
- How well does your database map to target customer personas?
- If you are using ABM methods, does your database map to ABM company targets?

Handling Resistance And Objections

As a marketing leader, you may get pushback from company leadership, sales, and even other marketing team members. Show stakeholders the facts, such as funnel conversion metrics or conversions where the first touch came from marketing programs.

Marketing is the lifeblood of any company. The above audit process ensures a company's marketing arteries stay clear and the blood keeps pumping.

Although it may be daunting to set up the process and templates the first time, you should be able to complete subsequent audits in one to two weeks, depending on the size of your organization.

MAKING THE RIGHT MARKETING MOVES
Audit Is Not A Dirty Word

1. **Get auditing.** Your company's success relies on the quality of your marketing strategy and tactical execution. Whether drafting a marketing budget of $25,000 or $250 million, a structured audit process ensures you learn lessons and make the required changes to max ROI every year.

2. **Set marketing KPIs you can measure against every year.** Document what worked and what didn't. Don't be afraid to kill programs that failed. Own the failure and move on. Marketing is about testing.

3. **Don't forget about resources.** Your team and its makeup are as important to measure as lead-generation campaigns. If you are bloated, cut. If you need more people to get the desired results, fight for them.

4. **Conduct an audit every year.** Quarterly is too often. An annual audit a couple of months before budget approval cycles is perfectly adequate.

5. **Share the audit results with chief financial officers.** CFOs love numbers and data. They will be impressed at this level of rigor coming from marketing and will be more likely to approve funding requests.

Move 23

BOLDLY GO INTO YOUR TECH
SUCCESS FUTURE

To boldly go where no one has gone before.

The words sound like something President John Kennedy would say. But if you are a science fiction geek like me, you know it was actually popularized by the 1960s TV show *Star Trek.*

The phrase has been attributed to Samuel A. Peeples, a prolific television writer best known for his Westerns.

The expression made its way into pop culture via the voiceover by Captain James T. Kirk (played by William Shatner), which opened every episode of the original run of the show:

> Space: the final frontier. These are the voyages of the starship Enterprise. Its five-year mission: to explore strange new worlds. To seek out new life and new civilizations. To boldly go where no man has gone before.

Of course, I prefer the series *Star Trek: The Next Generation* (1987–1994), which changed the wording to "boldly go where no one has gone before" to be more gender neutral.[54] Or *Star Trek: Voyager*, because who can beat the first woman captain, Kathryn Janeway.

THE BOLD AND BRAVE
WORLD OF MARKETING

Marketing, like space exploration, is for the brave. It's finger paint mixed with logic—a true meld of left- and right-brained skills. Great marketing teams are a combination of orators, mathematicians, and artists, just like the Enterprise had leaders, translators, scientists, and counselors.

On the one hand, marketing requires a deep understanding of data and analytics to measure the success of marketing efforts, allocate resources effectively, and make informed decisions.

On the other hand, it requires a level of creativity and intuition to generate fresh ideas, craft compelling messages, and engage with customers in meaningful ways.

Marketing requires strength and flexibility with a team that constantly adapts to changing customer needs and market conditions. It requires a willingness to take risks and try new things, knowing that not every campaign will be a success.

However, the rewards of successful marketing are unparalleled. By striking the right balance between analytics and creativity, companies can build strong relationships with their customers, establish a distinct brand identity, and drive growth and success for their business. The success stories in this book show that feeding, versus starving, your marketing is the key to growth.

AND IN CLOSING

I did not intend this book to be one that can be read quickly and immediately thoroughly absorbed. This is not the kind of marketing book that glorifies one single strategy or tactic.

But then again, scoring the next marketing triumph in the health tech, IT, or biotech space is not something you wake up one morning and decide to do, without giving it any prior thought.

This book outlines, and I do mean outlines, a total transformation of your marketing, including your mindset. Transformation doesn't happen overnight. And it's not easy to ponder in one sitting, either.

After you've read through this book (I said read, not skimmed), my suggestion is for you to go back and examine the moves chapter by chapter. Mark it up. Write in the margins. Use it as a workbook, a journal, an idea file.

I have seen the methods and principles in this book work time and time again. My clients have achieved explosive growth, and so can you.

I wish you success on your journey. Here are the power moves.

Avoid Starvation Marketing. You can't get to the top on the cheap.

Don't Bet On Just The Best Tech. Thinking the best tech will win in the end is a sucker bet.

Get Busy Marketing Or Get Busy Dying. Understand the growth imperative of business because your competitors do.

Build Your Marketing Tower Of Power. The better the foundation, the taller the tower.

Your Brand Can't Be Bland. There is a marketing axiom: you can't bore people into buying.

Know Your Who And What Their Pain Is. Find a niche and scratch their itch.

Write Your Company's Award Speech Today. Work with the end in mind and what will be your legacy.

Understand That Features And Benefits Don't Sell Hearts And Minds. Human brains are hardwired to make decisions on emotions, not facts and figures.

Failing To Create A Marketing Plan Is Planning To Fail. When was seat-of-the-pants or faking it until you make it ever a good strategy?

Build A Better Budget That Gets Buy-In. Committed money is the rocket fuel you need to reach the stars.

Build a Digital Mansion, Not An Online Shack. If you were an astronaut, would you want to be on a rocket built by the bargain bidder? Same goes for your website.

Believe That Content Is The Entire Back Row Of The Chessboard. Content is the secret marketing weapon that will win the chess game called business.

Find Ways To Generate More Content Without Bots. Content good; mindless bots bad in the long run. Bots aren't evil, just stupid. Use them wisely.

Get Out Your Megaphone. Nothing is more cost-effective at building visibility than great publicity.

Choose Your Business's Three Spokespeople. Usually, great publicity opportunities only knock once.

Fill Your Pipeline With Lead Generation. Think about leads like at-bats in a baseball game or shots on goal in soccer.

Hire Your Right Marketing Department. The best talent doesn't always prevail, but that's the way to wager.

Make Friends With Agencies. They can give you two valuable things: experience and consistency.

Think About Outsourcing Your Marketing. The outsourcing marketing model can be a game changer if you have the right mindset.

Market Like Athletes, Not Weekend Warriors. Consistency trumps feverish activity.

Practice Patience As A Marketing Virtue. The truth is that quality takes time.

Know That Audit Is Not A Dirty Word. As the proverb states: spending is quick, and earning is slow. So be sure to count the costs.

MAKING THE RIGHT MARKETING MOVES
Last Words For Leaders

1. **Praise and reward your marketing teams.**
   They are warriors on the front line every day constantly adapting to customer needs and market conditions. They need to tap right-brained and left-brained skills daily.

2. **Fund marketing budgets at a level to support business goals and failures.** If the marketing team can show the expected ROI, give them a baseline budget and room to test. Not every campaign works on the first try. But with testing and practice, your team can focus on what works.

3. **Give your marketing leader the same rank as your sales leader.** If you hire a chief commercial officer and marketing manager, you are immediately setting up a dynamic where sales has rank and power over marketing. When 80 percent of the purchase is decided before talking to a salesperson, why would you do this?

4. **Don't immediately dismiss agencies.** If you go into a partnership with the right mindset, communicate clear goals, and provide feedback, agencies can work wonders in a short time frame. I've seen resounding successes from well-crafted hybrid teams of agencies and in-house, and also of completely outsourced, marketing.

APPENDIX

ACKNOWLEDGEMENTS

To the dream team at Clarity Quest and all our clients, past and present, I could not have written this book without you. The success stories told are yours. I have the most fulfilling job in the world thanks to your creativity, intelligence, and humor. You've taught me the most valuable lessons of all: empathy and confident humility.

To my husband Ron, who always supports me doing unconventional things like quitting my job and starting an agency: I'd boldly and lovingly go with you anywhere in the universe.

To my daughter, who has infinite patience with Mom always needing "just one more minute." Thanks for sharing me with my dream and for turning out so creative and amazing despite your type A mom. Mommy and Marissa days forever.

To my mom, who is one of the fiercest woman warriors I know, and my brother who has one of the kindest hearts, thanks for your support and humor.

Finally, to my editor Henry DeVries, the word artist, I can't thank you enough for your wisdom, humor, and deadlines. Without you, the ideas in this book would still be sitting on my Google Drive.

ABOUT THE AUTHOR

Christine Slocumb, MSEE, MBA, has thirty years of marketing, business development, and product management experience in a wide variety of tech companies, from start-ups to Fortune 50 firms. Since founding Clarity Quest in 2001, she has worked with technology, life sciences, and healthcare firms on marketing strategy, business planning, and marketing implementation.

She has experience leading in-house marketing and agency client services teams, developing processes, managing marketing operations, and owning P&L responsibilities. She believes the marketing function must be accountable for producing tangible results and positive ROI.

Slocumb holds eight US patents and is a member of the Forbes Agency Council. She's an avid paddler and an addicted golfer.

WORKS CITED AND AUTHOR'S NOTES

1   "AIDA," Oxford Reference, accessed April 3, 2023, https://www.ox-fordreference.com/display/10.1093/oi/authority.20110803095432783;
jsessionid=029358AD8585B14F9FFC363F348BB695.

2   Greg Sterling, "B2B Buyers Consume An Average Of 13 Content Pieces Before Deciding On A Vendor," MarTech.org, February 14, 2020, https://martech.org/b2b-buyers-consume-an-average-of-13-content-pieces-before-deciding-on-a-vendor/.

3   Rama Ramaswami, "Future Of Sales 2025: Deliver The Digital Options B2B Buyers Demand," Gartner.com, March 10, 2021, https://www.gartner.com/smarterwithgartner/future-of-sales-2025-deliver-the-digital-options-b2b-buyers-demand.

4   "Longer Sales, Greater Expectations, Less Contact," Considered.com, accessed April 3, 2023, https://considered.prolific.li/longer-sales-report/.

5   "Longer Sales," Considered.com.

6   US Attorney's Office, Northern District of California, "Theranos Founder Elizabeth Holmes Found Guilty Of Investor Fraud," press release, updated April 19, 2023, https://www.justice.gov/usao-ndca/pr/theranos-founder-elizabeth-holmes-found-guilty-investor-fraud. Elizabeth A. Holmes, the founder of blood testing company Theranos, Inc., was convicted in 2022 of defrauding investors of hundreds of millions of dollars. According to the US Attorney's Office, Holmes made false representations to investors and potential investors about the company's blood testing product and made numerous misrepresentations to potential investors about Theranos's financial condition and its future prospects.

7   Latané Conant, *No Forms. No Spam. No Cold Calls.* (San Francisco: 6sense Insights, Inc., 2020).

8   "The CMO Survey: Managing and Measuring Marketing Spending For Growth And Returns," Deloitte, August 2021, https://cmosurvey.org/wp-content/uploads/2021/08/The_CMO_Survey-Highlights_and_Insights_Report-August_2021.pdf.

9   "How CMOs Are Spending Their Marketing Budget–And What It Means For You," Gartner.com, accessed April 3, 2023, https://www.gartner.com/en/marketing/research/annual-cmo-spend-sur-vey-research.

10 Picture archiving and communications systems (PACSs) are what hospitals use to store, digitally transmit, and manage images.

11 "IDC MarketScape Report Names Mach7 A Leader In U.S. Healthcare Provider VNA/AICA Unstructured Data Platforms For Integrated Care," Businesswire.com, June 7, 2016, https://www.businesswire.com/news/home/20160607005592/en/IDC-Market-Scape-Report-Names-Mach7-a-Leader-in-U.S.-Healthcare-Provid-er-VNAAICA-Unstructured-Data-Platforms-for-Integrated-Care.

12 "Universal Imaging (Viewer) Best In Klas 2023," Klasresearch.com, accessed April 3, 2023, https://klasresearch.com/best-in-klas-ranking/universal-viewer-imaging/2023/305.

13 Simon Sinek, *Start With Why: How Great Leaders Inspire Everyone To Take Action* (London: Portfolio Publishing, 2009).

14 FedEx is a registered trademark of the FedEx Corporation. The FedEx trademark is a syllabic abbreviation of the original name from the air division that was named Federal Express until 2000. FedEx is organized into different operating units and each operating unit has its own version of the trademark, which makes it an ideal example.

15 Sally Hogshead, *Fascinate: How to Make Your Brand Impossible to Resist*, rev. ed. (New York: Harper Business Publishers, 2016). Branding expert Sally Hogshead says: "It's good to be better but better to be different."

16 Josh Steimle, "What CMOs Need To Know About Buyer Personas," Forbes.com, August 18, 2015, https://www.forbes.com/sites/josh-steimle/2015/08/18/what-cmos-need-to-know-about-buyer-per-sonas/?sh=137bd5c83135.

17 Marty Neumeier, *ZAG: The #1 Strategy Of High-Performance Brands* (Indianapolis, IN: New Riders, 2006).

18 Ann Handley, *Everybody Writes: Your New and Improved Go-To Guide To Creating Ridiculously Good Content*, 2nd ed. (Hoboken, NJ: John Wiley & Sons, 2022).

19 For more, read Nancy Harhut, *Using Behavioral Science in Marketing* (New York: Kogan Page, 2022).

20 "The CMO Survey," Deloitte.

21 In Henry DeVries, "Three Must-Have Stories To Grow Your Business," Forbes.com, May 22, 2022.

22 Earnings Before Interest, Taxes, Depreciation, and Amortization, or EBITDA, is a financial metric that measures an organization's operating profitability.

23 "The Four Ps Of Marketing: What They Are And How To Use Them," Coursera, updated August 10, 2022, https://www.coursera.org/articles/4-ps-of-marketing.

24 Jon Miller, "The CMO's Guide To Setting And Defending Your Marketing Budget And ROI," Demandbase, February 14, 2023, https://www.demandbase.com/blog/setting-and-defending-marketing-budget-and-roi/.

25 "The CMO Survey," Deloitte, p. 30.

26 Jason Wise, "How Many Google Searches Per Day In 2023?," Earthweb.com, updated May 10, 2023, https://earthweb.com/how-many-google-searches-per-day/.

27 "How To Use AI And Automation To Eliminate Coding Errors," *BC Advantage*, September/October 2022, https://www.billing-coding.com/currentissue.cfm.

28 "The Propel Media Barometer—Q1 2023," Propel, accessed April 3, 2023, https://www.propelmypr.com/research/the-propel-media-barometer-q1-2023.

29 Lauren Hirsch, "Companies Desperate To Reopen Ask: What's Your Vaccination Status?," *New York Times*, June 11, 2021, https://www.nytimes.com/2021/06/11/business/vaccines-companies-offices.html.

30 *2023 Edelman Trust Barometer*, Edelman Trust Institute, https://www.edelman.com/sites/g/files/aatuss191/files/2023-03/2023%20Edelman%20Trust%20Barometer%20Global%20Report%20FINAL.pdf.

31 Winston S. Churchill, "The Scaffolding of Rhetoric," November 1897, International Churchill Society, Accessed April 3, 2023, https://winstonchurchill.org/churchill-central/image/the-scaffolding-of-rhetoric-3/.

32 We only use this traditional funnel for calculated number of engaged prospects we need. This is not how people actually buy, as explained in the preface.

33 Series C financing (also known as series C round or series C funding) is one of the stages in the capital-raising process by a start-up. The series C round is the fourth stage of start-up financing, and typically the last stage of venture-capital financing. However, some companies opt to conduct more rounds, such as series D, E, or beyond.

34 A/B testing, alternatively called split testing, involves a random-ized experimental procedure where multiple variations of a variable (such as a web page or ad design) are simultaneously presented to distinct groups of website visitors. The purpose is to identify the version that generates the most significant impact and improves business metrics.

35 "Average Chief Marketing Office (CMO) Salary," Payscale, accessed May 21, 2023 https://www.payscale.com/research/US/Job=Chief_Marketing_Officer_(CMO)/Salary

36 "How much does a Chief Marketing Officer (CO) make?," Glassdoor, accessed May14, 2023, https://www.glassdoor.com/Salaries/united-states-chief-marketing-officer-cmo-salary-SRCH_IL.0,13_IN1_KO14,41.htm

37 "Average Content Marketing Manager," Payscale, Accessed May 21, 2023, https://www.payscale.com/research/US/Job=Content_Marketing_Manager/Salary

38 "How much does a Content Marketing Manager make?," Glassdoor, accessed May 14, 2023, https://www.glassdoor.com/Salaries/us-content-marketing-manager-salary-SRCH_IL.0,2_IN1_KO3,28.htm

39 "Average Marketing Technology Manager Salary." Payscale, accessed May 21, 2023https://www.payscale.com/research/US/Job=Marketing_Technology_Manager/Salary

40 "How much does a Marketing Technology Manager make?," Glassdoor, accessed May 14, 2023, https://www.glassdoor.com/Salaries/us-marketing-technology-manager-salary-SRCH_IL.0,2_IN1_KO3,31.htm

41 "Average Marketing Director Salary," Payscale, accessed May 21, 2023, https://www.payscale.com/research/US/Job=Marketing_Director/Salary

42 "How much does a Marketing Director make?," Glassdoor, accessed May 14, 2023, https://www.glassdoor.com/Salaries/us-marketing-technology-manager-salary-SRCH_IL.0,2_IN1_KO3,31.htm

43 "Average Marketing Strategist Salary," Payscale, accessed May 21, 2023, https://www.payscale.com/research/US/Job=Marketing_Strategist/Salary

44 "How much does a Marketing Strategist make?," Glassdoor, accessed May 14, 2023, https://www.glassdoor.com/Salaries/us-marketing-technology-manager-salary-SRCH_IL.0,2_IN1_KO3,31.htm

45 "Average Marketing Analyst Salary," Payscale, accessed May 21, 2023, https://www.payscale.com/research/US/Job=Marketing_Analyst/Salary

46 "How much does a Marketing-Analyst make?," Glassdoor, accessed May 14, 2023, https://www.glassdoor.com/Salaries/us-marketing-technology-manager-salary-SRCH_IL.0,2_IN1_KO3,31.htm

47 "Average Graphic Designer Salary," Payscale, accessed May 21, 2023, https://www.payscale.com/research/US/Job=Graphic_Designer/Salary

48 "How much does a Graphic Designer make?," Glassdoor, accessed May 14, 2023, https://www.glassdoor.com/Salaries/us-marketing-technology-manager-salary-SRCH_IL.0,2_IN1_KO3,31.htm

49 "Average Digital Marketing Manager Salary," Payscale, accessed May 21, 2023, https://www.payscale.com/research/US/Job=Digital_Marketing_Manager/Salary

50 "How much does a Marketing Technology Manager make?," Glassdoor, accessed May 14, 2023, https://www.glassdoor.com/Salaries/us-marketing-technology-manager-salary-SRCH_IL.0,2_IN1_KO3,31.htm

51 Forrester, "Transformation Goes Pragmatic," Forbes.com, November 9, 2018, https://www.forbes.com/sites/forrester/2018/11/09/transformation-goes-pragmatic/?sh=5a35a55947c9.

52 Paul H. Falcone, Chih-Yin Tai, Laura R. Carson, Jordan M. Joy, et.al., "Caloric Expenditure of Aerobic, Resistance, or Combined High-Intensity Interval Training Using a Hydraulic Resistance System in Healthy Men," *Journal of Strength and Conditioning Research* 29(3):p 779-785, March 2015, Caloric Expenditure of Aerobic, Resistance, or Combined High... : The Journal of Strength & Conditioning Research (lww.com)

53 Rayna Southart, "The Countdown To HIMSS Is On! Are You Getting Ready?," Clarity Quest, September 13, 2022, https://www.clarityqst.com/blog/the-countdown-to-himss-is-on-are-you-getting-ready/.

54 "Words We Know Because Of Star Trek," Dictionary.com, June 5, 2020, https://www.dictionary.com/e/star-trek-words/.

INDEX

.

www.ingramcontent.com/pod-product-compliance
Lightning Source LLC
Chambersburg PA
CBHW040855210326
41597CB00029B/4853